Self-Sufficiency

Breadmaking

Self-Sufficiency

Breadmaking

Kathryn Hawkins

NEW
HOLLAND

First published in 2012 by New Holland Publishers (UK) Ltd
London • Cape Town • Sydney • Auckland

Garfield House	Wembley Square	Unit 1, 66 Gibbes St	218 Lake Road
86–88 Edgware Rd	Solan Street, Gardens	Chatswood	Northcote
London W2 2EA	Cape Town 8000	NSW 2067	Auckland
United Kingdom	South Africa	Australia	New Zealand

ISBN 978 1 78009 041 2

Publisher: Clare Sayer
Senior Editor: Marilyn Inglis
Designer: Peter Crump
Production: Laurence Poos
Illustrations: David Sparshott

2 4 6 8 10 9 7 5 3 1

Reproduction by Pica Digital PTE Ldt, Singapore
Printed and bound in China by Toppan Leefung Printing Ltd

CONTENTS

INTRODUCTION

Making bread is truly fascinating. A few very simple ingredients – flour, water and yeast – once given the correct conditions and care, work together to provide something most of us eat and enjoy every single day of our lives. Bread is something anyone can afford to make; it's achievable with only a basic level of culinary skill and you only have to follow a few simple rules.

The process of making the dough itself is often regarded as therapeutic – there's nothing better for relieving a bit of tension than thumping and kneading the dough on the work surface – and adapting a recipe by adding extra ingredients and shaping the dough to fit your requirements unleashes your creative side. Filling your kitchen with the delicious smells of fresh baking heightens the senses and then, of course, the finished product tastes great. Bread is the staple food of many diets the world over and making your own means you are able to provide an enjoyable and nutritious food for your family and your guests.

This book gives anyone who is interested in making their own bread a good grounding in all the essential constituents that combine to make the perfect loaf. You'll find a guide to the ingredients that make up the average loaf, as well as a simple explanation of their role in making up the dough. This is followed by an in-depth look at the different stages involved in breadmaking. It might look a bit daunting at first glance but it really is very straightforward once you get going. Just a few simple guidelines and you'll be well on your way to creating your own delicious bread.

Once you've read through the basics, you'll find the all-important recipe section. These pages should provide you with instructions for all the basic loaves you might want to bake, from the plain white loaf to the more luxurious enriched breads such as brioche and stöllen. There are a couple of recipes for gluten-free baking as well as yeast-free loaves, and throughout this section you'll find hints and tips for making variations in flavour, texture and shape. The best news about breadmaking is that you don't need any fancy equipment. You should be able to get started right away and will soon be enjoying the aroma of fresh baking and the unbeatable taste of wholesome, freshly made bread.

A brief history

Bread is a fundamental food throughout the world. This simple everyday staple, referred to as 'the staff of life', has provided vital sustenance for humans since the beginning of time. In times of hardship, individuals have often survived on bread and water alone, and in times of celebration, bread is always part of the feast.

Bread from prehistory to the 21st century

Bread has been at the centre of culinary and cultural life for humans since prehistoric times, and it has played a role in religious customs and superstitions for centuries. In Christian tradition, the 'breaking of bread' during Holy Communion symbolizes the body of Christ. Traditionally loaves were hung in houses on Good Friday to ward off evil spirits and a cross was cut into the top of breads as a ritual to 'let the Devil out'. Special breads are baked for specific occasions: hot cross buns for Easter; Jewish matzo for Passover, and harvest loaves to signify fertility and abundance for the year ahead.

The evolution of our humble loaf goes hand in hand with developments in raising crops, milling and baking. In Europe, West Asia and the Near East, suitable grains such as wheat, rye and barley, thrive. Where the climate is less suitable for these grains, other crops such as rice have become the staple of choice.

For thousands of years grains were ground into a type of flour by using a pestle and mortar-type utensil to give roughly ground grain. This process was superseded by the use of two flat stones pressing against each other to produce a finer-grained flour. Referred to as 'saddle stones', this method is represented in Egyptian hieroglyphs and mill stones have been excavated in many parts of the world. In prehistoric times, the simple flours produced were mixed with water and cooked in the fire or on hot stones to make hard flat breads.

This foodstuff was a common part of the diet in late Stone-Age life in parts of the world where grain grew well, and these early breads survive today – puri, roti, chapati and tortillas are all forms of this ancient cooking method.

The Egyptians are credited with discovering the process of leavening bread, although they probably discovered it by accident. No doubt a batch of simple dough was left out in the warmth and became contaminated with wild yeasts in the air – it is worth remembering that the brewing of beer and wine was also an important part of ancient Egyptian culinary life. This caused the dough to ferment and rise and when baked, the resulting bread was lighter in texture and tasted much better than the usual flat-baked loaves. Soon they discovered that a piece of this fermented dough could be added to another batch to give the same result. By 2000 BC, bread had become so popular in Egypt that there is evidence of a professional baking industry, producing leavened as well as the traditional flat breads. When the Israelites fled Egypt, they left behind their leavened bread and thus the origin of the Passover unleavened matzo became part of the tradition of that religious observance.

Wheat wasn't grown in Greece and the North Mediterranean until about 400 BC, but the people in this part of the world soon developed a refining process and prided themselves in making 'white' loaves fit for the gods. They also added seeds, fruit, nuts and enriched their loaves with oliv oil. The spread of the Roman Empire saw the real development of breadmaking. Out went the less reliable spontaneous fermentation processes of the Egyptians; the bread industry became reliant on the use of brewers' yeast, a technique picked up from the Gauls who added beer to their doughs, and the partnership between bakehouse and brewhouse was forged. Bread in its many shapes and forms was a central feature of culinary life in late Roman times and wheat exportation hit the big time.

There was a thriving bakery trade throughout Europe by the Middle Ages. Specialist bakers produced whole-grain traditional loaves as well as more refined and luxurious white bread. There were loaves produced to suit all levels of society: 'hall' bread for the property owners; hulled bread made from bran for the servants; well-cooked, crusty wholemeal loaves for eating; and trenchers – dense, thick flat breads – were used as plates during medieval feasts. Many large properties of the time had their own in-house bakery alongside their own brewery.

Fancy breads and pastries became popular during
the Renaissance, and domestic recipes began to appear in cookbooks
of the time. During the 18th century, agricultural systems further
evolved and one of the consequences was a more refined flour;
the introduction of silk sieves made possible a more powdery form
of flour. Bakers were also able to use brewers' and distillers' yeasts
as ingredients added directly to bread mixtures rather than the
traditional technique of adding a piece of fermented dough.

The Industrial Revolution in the 18th and 19th centuries
brought with it many social changes in society – the increase
in job opportunities in towns and cities took people away
from rural areas and with their new-found sources of
income they were able to spend more on food. In food
production, revolutionary steel roller mills arrived in
the 1870s that were able to produce white flour at
speed on a large scale and gradually the old coal
ovens were replaced with efficient gas ones
that helped speed up baking processes.

The 20th century saw many advances in the breadmaking process including bleaching flour to make it whiter (and seemingly more appealing and the requirement to enrich white flour with calcium, iron and vitamin Once rationing ended in the mid-20th century, the consumption of foods high in fats and sugars rose in popularity, and to meet demand, the baker industry expanded and became mechanized on a large scale. Most notabl the development of the Chorleywood Bread Process (CBP) in the 1960s speeded up the whole industry by developing a factory procedure using lower-grade wheat, more yeast and more chemical ingredients in combination with rapid fermentation and high-speed mechanized dough mixing. Factories were able to produce softer, less crusty loaves, which were readily available and affordable. This mass-produced bread lasted several days and provided a cheap filler to bulk out more expensive food such as meat, fish and dairy products. Once women went out to work, few had time to make their own loaves, so we became reliant on commercially produced bread.

However, some 50 years later, a resurgence in baking has begun. Once we became more concerned about what we were eating in relation to health, a drive to reduce fat, sugar and salt content in our everyday foods began. Consumers began to demand better flavour, texture and quality from their daily bread. Concerns abou the use of pesticides in wheat production and artificial additives used during the bread- making process prompted a return to more traditional types of flour. Advances in medical research helped more easily diagnose the condition Coeliac diseas (an intolerance to wheat and gluten Manufacturers began to change the way they produced breads and more organic, less refined and gluten-free loaves appeared on the shelves at the local bakers, corner shops and supermarkets.

When the domestic mechanical bread machine was invented in Japan in the late 1980s, this also contributed to the way we viewed our daily loaf. Soon many homes had this appliance and we were back to baking bread in a fraction of the time it took to make it by hand.

In recent years, artisan bakeries have sprung up and more bakers are making traditional recipes again. With the rise in popularity of farmers' markets, farm shops and specialist delicatessens, bread has become more exotic and flavoursome. As is often the way, this sparked off an interest in the domestic setting, and home cooks have begun making their own bread from scratch. More and more of us are spending time in the kitchen resurrecting the recipes our grandparents used to make, enjoying baking and creating all sorts of delicious goodies with the wealth of wonderful ingredients we have available to us.

Breads from around the world

A visit to any bakers' shop, deli or in-store supermarket bakery can be a mind-boggling experience these days. There are loaves of all shapes and sizes, different textures, toppings and flavours, sweet and savoury; from plain everyday bread to the fancy and outlandish, you'll find a loaf suit every occasion. Sitting alongside your average white or wholemeal loaf you'll find breads from around the world. Some of these loaves use grains other than wheat – rye bread (page 98), for example, are popular Germany and Scandinavia. Some use a sourdough starter instead of more conventional yeast – Italian Ciabatta (page 96) is one of the most popular type of sourdough bread we eat today.

As well as the familiar breads we cut up and slice, there are many varieties of flat bread, some leavened with yeast such as naan and pitta (pages 108 and 106), and others that contain no yeast, which are the most like the original flat loaves. For special occasions, enriched breads make a delicious treat. French brioche (page 102) is especially rich with eggs, butter and sugar added to the dough, and the festive Italian panettone loaf (page 110), baked in a tall round tin, has the flavour of vanilla with added finely chopped fruit peel and vine fruits.

For the health-conscious or those on special diets, there are all sorts of breads with added extra fibre, nuts and seeds, and mixtures made without gluten. People with a wheat or gluten intolerance have to avoid ordinary breads, but making bread without gluten presents a challenge to the baker.

The chewy texture that wheat protein imparts to the finished loaf is difficult to achieve without wheat in the dough. Xanthan gum (a natural by-product formed by a strain of bacteria feeding on sugars) is often used with gluten-free grains to help achieve a more acceptable elastic texture. Gluten-free breads can also be made without xanthan gum or yeast by using a raising agent such as baking powder – you'll find recipes covering both methods on pages 90 and 124. These breads have a more 'cakey' or scone-like texture, and have a shorter keeping quality, but they do make a good alternative to going without bread altogether.

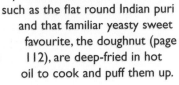

Not all breads rely only on oven baking. Traditional French baguettes are cooked with a source of steam in the oven to help achieve the soft, fluffy crumb and chewy, crusty exterior (page 92); before baking, Jewish bagels are first cooked in water to puff up the dough and form the soft interior, which forms the familiar golden crust (page 104). The Chinese have been making and eating steamed buns for centuries. These breads are small, round, shiny and white with a chewy texture and are made from fermented soft wheat or barley dough. Many of the flat breads, made with and without yeast, are dry-cooked in a hot pan on the stove; other breads such as the flat round Indian puri and that familiar yeasty sweet favourite, the doughnut (page 112), are deep-fried in hot oil to cook and puff them up.

Essential ingredients

The archetypal loaf is made from a mixture of flour, water and yeast, with a little seasoning. The type of flour you use, along with other variations in ingredients will affect the final outcome. The following pages offer a comprehensive guide to the different types of flour, yeasts and liquids you can use, as well as other ingredients that can be added to enrich, flavour and give texture to your breads.

The staff of life – wheat

Wheat flour is the most commonly used flour in breadmaking, but there are a few useful things to know about the grain itself before you go in search of breadmaking flour.

Wheat kernel or berry

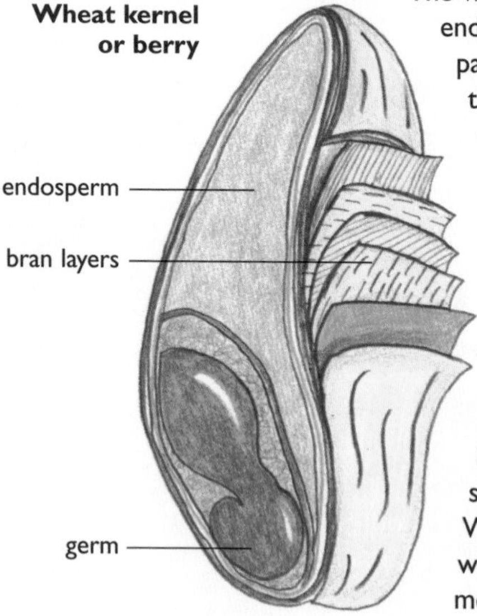

endosperm

bran layers

germ

The wheat grain is made up of bran layers, germ and endosperm. The bran is the husky fibrous outer part of the grain consisting of seven layers, and the germ is the nutritious seed. Right in the centre is the endosperm, which is full of starch and protein, and makes up the bulk of berry. While there are several different proteins in the endosperm, the two most important for breadmaking are *gliadin* and *glutenin*. When these two come into contact with moisture and get stirred up in a mixture, they produce the sticky substance gluten, which gives elasticity to bread dough and helps hold up the basic structure of the loaf during cooking. Wheat flours, made from varieties of wheat with a high protein content of 12 percent or more, will make the best-textured bread. These high-protein flours contain more of the proteins that make gluten and are made from hard grain varieties of wheat.

heat flours

While professional bakers can obtain flours made from specific types of wheat grain, most flours on sale to the domestic cook are labelled according to their specific use in the kitchen. Some are suitable for breadmaking, while others are used for cakes and biscuits. Compositions can vary considerably so read the labels on the packet to obtain as much information about the type of flour you are buying before you start your breadmaking. Here are a few general types of wheat flour explained:

Plain white flour
A traditional multi-purpose wheat flour milled from soft wheat grains with a protein content between 7 and 10 percent. This flour is best for cake and pastry-making and soft-textured unleavened breads where a spongy, soft texture is required. You can mix this flour with flour that has a higher protein content to increase the suitability for breadmaking.

Wholemeal plain flour
While this wholesome flour contains all the grain, bran and germ, and has more protein than its refined white cousin, the protein comes from the germ protein rather than from gluten. Therefore, use this one in the same way as plain white.

Bread flour
Also called **strong** and **very strong bread flour**, this is the flour of choice for breadmaking and is available as a white or wholemeal flour. These flours are made from hard wheat varieties that naturally contain more gluten and an overall protein content between 12 and 14 percent depending

on the manufacturer. Wholemeal bread flour is made with the whole wheat kernel and has more fibre, but using all wholemeal bread flour to make a loaf will give a dense, heavy texture since the extra bran content inhibits the ability to develop gluten during kneading. You may want to combine white and wholemeal to obtain an acceptable texture. I have included some ratios on page 26 to give you some guidance.

Brown flour

Also called **wheatmeal**, this is a lighter, less fibre-rich version of wholemeal flour, with some of the wheat bran removed. It contains most of the wheat germ, so is still of good nutritional quality. It will make a lighter loaf than one made entirely of wholemeal.

Soft-grain strong bread flour

White bread flour with added kibbled or cracked wheat and rye grains t add texture, this flour makes an excellent halfway measure in the battle t get more dietary fibre into the diet without the heaviness achieved by using 100 percent wholewheat flour. Kids love it too!

Granary malted brown bread flour

Also called **country grain**, **malted wheatgrain** and **malthouse** flour, this delicious bread flour with added malted wheat flakes gives a nutty texture and sweet flavou to breads.

Semolina flour

This can be coarse ground or finely ground (in which case it known as durum flour and is used in pasta-making). Milled from strain called durum wheat, it is one of the hardest varieties. When mixed with white bread flour it makes a slightly coarser-textured, more rustic loaf with good flavour and a creamy yellow crumb.

Spelt flour

This flour is becoming more widely available, and is made from an ancient type of wheat grain that was certainly used by the Romans. *Triticum spelta* wheat has a lower gluten content than many modern-day commercial wheat varieties, and when it is milled, the flour is lighter than traditional wholemeal flours. You may also find a white spelt flour, which gives still lighter results. While it makes a cakier-textured loaf when used on its own, the flavour is delicious and the texture can be improved by mixing it with strong white bread flour if you prefer.

Non-wheat flours

No other cereal crop contains as much vital gluten as wheat, but since breadmaking began, people have been grinding other grains to put with their wheat flour to lend variety, bulk and different textures to their bread baking.

Rye flour

A hardy grain that tolerates wet and cold climates hence its popularity in Russian, Scandanavian and North European cookery, rye contains some gluten and if used on its own makes a very heavy bread with a distinctly acidic flavour. For most palettes, it is better mixed with wheat flour for a lighter loaf.

Buckwheat flour
Also known as **beechwheat**, **brank** or **Saracen corn**, these greyish triangular grains come from a plant native to Russia; it is related to rhubarb, not wheat. Buckwheat is a gluten-free, nutritious grain containing rutin, which is used as a natural remedy for circulatory problems. When ground into flour, it has a nutty, earthy flavour, and should be mixed with wheat flour for making bread. Buckwheat can also be used in gluten-free baking (see page 26).

Oat flour
Cleaned and hulled oat grains are called **groats**, and these can be ground finely to make a tasty, nutritious and fibre-rich flour. Pure uncontaminated oats naturally contain no gluten, but often oats are processed on premises where other gluten-containing grains are handled. If you have Coeliac disease, always read the product label for suitability. Oat flour can be mixed with wheat flour to give a richer texture to a loaf.

Barley flour
Once the husky bran is removed from barley grains it becomes pearl or pot barley, which is a familiar ingredient in stews and soups. Pearl barley is ground to make a delicious sweet, earthy flour that is gluten-free.

Quinoa
Although not really a grain, quinoa is often treated as one; it produces protein-rich seeds with a high concentration of amino acids. It hails from South America and is a valuable crop in this part of the world as it grows at altitudes too high for the maize crop. It is gluten-free and has little flavour but is used with wheat flour in breadmaking to enhance the nutritional quality of the finished loaf.

Gram flour
Also called **chickpea flour** and **garbanzo bean flour**, it is made by grinding chickpeas into a golden, powdery flour. It contains no gluten but has a rich earthy flavour, which is best suited to savoury breads. In Indian cookery it is used to make pancakes, bhajis and flat breads such as chapatis. A little goes a long way when mixed with wheat flour to give a rich beany flavour.

Potato flour
A very starchy, pure-white grainy flour made from potato starch, this contains no gluten and is used in small quantities with wheat bread flour to soften a loaf and give a moist texture.

Soya flour
Milled from soybeans, this flour has a very high protein content; it is low in carbohydrate, contains no gluten and is used to enhance the nutritional content of a loaf. It also adds a creamier, softer texture to the crumb.

Cornmeal
Widely used as a staple grain in corn- (maize-) growing parts of the world, it is available in a variety of textures from very fine to coarse (polenta). Rich golden-yellow cornmeal contains no gluten and is often added to wheat flours in breadmaking, but is also mixed with other non-gluten flours to make dense soda breads (page 125).

Rice flour
Finely ground white or brown rice grains are used to make this variety of flour. It is very starchy, contains no gluten and is used in small amounts to lighten and soften the crumb. Brown rice flour will also add a little nutty flavour as well.

Gluten- and wheat-free bread flour

Several manufacturers produce their own blends of gluten-free flours to make life easier for the consumer. Combinations often include rice, buckwheat, corn, tapioca and potato flours mixed with a quantity of the natural binder xanthan gum (see page 29). Loaves made with gluten-free flour will not be the same as the traditional wheat loaf, and recipes are quite different. The texture is denser, more cake-like, and less crusty, but it makes an excellent alternative to going without bread altogether. It also saves time and money putting your own blends together.

Making your own bread flour blends

For the best results, use at least 50 percent bread flour in your loaf. If th other 50 percent of the flour quantity is made up of a gluten-free flour, t loaf will still rise, but the texture will be far less chewy and springy than your usual all-wheat loaf.

I would recommend that the inexperienced breadmaker who wants t make a wholemeal loaf starts by making a loaf with 50 percent white bread flour and 50 percent wholemeal. This will give a lightly fibred loaf with a good rise and a chewy texture. For a denser texture, move on to 75 percent wholemeal to 25 percent white brea flour. Once you have mastered this type of doug try making one with 100 percent wholemeal bread flour.

Using gluten-free flours such as gram, soya, buckwheat and rye, is down to personal taste, but as a general rule, replace 6–8 tbsp wheat flour with equal amounts of one of the above will make a subtle change to basic white bread (see page 78).

Bread flour blend tips

• Because rye flour does contain some gluten it can be used in larger quantities than other non-wheat grain flours, but the flavour is distinctly different and may not be as palatable if used in a higher ratio.
• Flours such as rice and potato are used to soften the texture of the crumb, and 4–6 tbsp should be sufficient to make a subtle difference.

east and other leavening agents

Just as important in breadmaking as the right type of flour is the leavening agent. This essential ingredient helps create the airy gases in the dough that make the bread rise. Yeast is the most commonly used ingredient for this purpose and it is available in three different forms.

Fresh yeast

This looks a bit like chunks of canned tuna. It is moist and soft in texture and smells fresh and slightly sweet. You may be able to obtain some from a local bakery, delicatessen and some supermarkets, but you can also get it online (see pages 124–125). It is best used as soon as possible after purchase to ensure it is fresh, otherwise keep it well wrapped up in the fridge and use according to the use-by date.

To use fresh yeast, mash it up with slightly warm liquid and stir until blended – full instructions are given on pages 46–47. If you bulk-buy fresh yeast, you can cut it into measured portions, wrap securely in clingfilm and freeze it until you need it (up to six months). It thaws very quickly and becomes liquid once defrosted. It can be activated in the same way as fresh yeast.

Dried yeast

Also known as **active dry baking yeast**, this ingredient is often sold in small resealable tins. A concentrated form of yeast, it keeps in a cool, dark cupboard for about two months once opened. It resembles tiny yellowish-brown seeds and like fresh yeast, it needs to be mixed with warm liquid in order to activate it; this process may take slightly longer than when using fresh (see page 46 for full instructions). If your recipe requires fresh yeast but you don't have any to hand, replace it with half the quantity of active dry yeast, but always check the manufacturer's instructions.

Easy-blend yeast
Also known as **quick yeast** or **fast-acting yeast**, this yeast is finer than dried yeast and is specially formulated so that it needs no pre-activating. is added directly to the flour and the liquid added to make the dough activates the yeast. Easy-blend is often available in ready-to-use one-portion (7 g) sachets, but also in larger packs. As a rough guide one 7 g sachet is equivalent to 15 g (½ oz) fresh yeast or 2 tsp dried yeast, but check the manufacturer's guidelines. Once opened, it doesn't keep that well and is best stored in a clean airtight container in a cool, dry place. Check the manufacturer's guidelines for storage times once opened.

Sourdough starter

There are numerous recipes and methods for this natural way of making bread rise. It is a lengthier process than using other leavening agents but once a starter is made it can be replenished and, providing it is stored correctly, you will have a continuous supply for your breadmaking. Loaves made with sourdough starter have a fresh, light acidic flavour, and a more aerated crumb. Flour and water are the basic ingredient of the starter and yeast may be added to ferment the mixture, but some starters are yeast-free. Other ingredients are sometimes added to sweeten and flavour the mixture. Keep your starter covered in the fridge (see page 47 for a basic recipe).

Other leaveners

While most bread doughs use yeast, some recipes for quick breads or those formulated for anyone on a special diet use other chemical leavens to get air into the mixture. They are usually stirred into the dry ingredient and liquid is added. Once moistened, these agents get to work quickly releasing the gases that help the mixture rise. Once mixed up, you have to bake the mixture quickly, otherwise the aeration will diminish.

Baking powder

This is a commercial mix of alkaline powder (bicarbonate of soda) and acid powder (cream of tartar) combined with a dried starch or wheat or rice flour to stabilize them. These two react together in the presence of moisture to make carbon dioxide gas, which helps the mixture rise. You can make your own baking powder by mixing 1 tbsp bicarbonate of soda with 2 tsp cream of tartar. Always measure using level spoon measurements unless otherwise stated – too much or too little can upset the balance of the recipe.

Bicarbonate of soda

This alkaline substance can be used on its own where an acid ingredient is present – buttermilk or lemon juice, for instance. This will help produce the same reaction achieved by using baking powder without adding extra acidity. It is worth noting that bicarbonate of soda has a salty flavour so you may want to reduce the salt in your mixture if adding it or baking powder to your recipe.

Xanthan gum

Also known as **corn sugar gum**, it has a food additive reference number E415; this rather scientific-sounding ingredient gets its name from bacteria used in the fermentation process. The bacteria form a natural slimy substance and this has been formulated for culinary use. Xanthan gum is widely used in gluten-free cooking to help improve crumb structure and also in dairy-free products as a natural binder (non-dairy ice cream). In breadmaking, you still need to use yeast, but the xanthan gum powder is mixed into the gluten-free flour before the liquid is added. You should be able to buy xanthan gum from large supermarkets, health food shops or stockists of special diet products. Always refer to the manufacturer's guidelines for quantities but as a general rule use 1 level tsp per 225 g (8 oz) gluten-free flour.

Liquid

The third key ingredient in breadmaking is a liquid of some sort; this gets the mixture going by bringing the flour together to make a stiff paste and developing the gluten to make a dough.

Depending on the method you use, your liquid is either a carrier for adding yeast to the mixture or an activator to help the leavening process get started. Water is most commonly used, giving the most chewy, familiar texture to a loaf. Milk, yoghurt or buttermilk can used, as can dairy-free soya, rice or coconut milk. The fat content of the liquid determines the texture of the finished crumb: the higher the fat, the more cake-like the crumb. Fruit and vegetable juices can also be used as the liquid in breadmaking, but you need to be mindful of the extra sugar you will be adding to the dough and make compensations to your recipe (see the notes on sugar opposite).

ther ingredients

Salt

As well as being an obvious flavour enhancer, salt acts as a brake mechanism in breadmaking. It prevents the yeast from overworking and causing the dough to collapse; in other words, it inhibits fermentation and allows the gluten to develop and strengthen, and form the structure of the loaf. Always measure salt carefully to avoid adding too much, and use natural sea salts rather than salt substitutes. Choose a finely ground salt or salt flakes rather than coarse, as they dissolve more quickly.

Sugar

A number of recipes, savoury as well as sweet, contain a sweetening agent either in the form of sugars, honey, syrup, malt extract, treacle or molasses. Traditionally, sugar is used to fuel fresh

yeast and speed up the fermentation process, but in fact, bread dough doesn't need sugar at all. However, adding a little will develop flavour and texture and help to form the crust. If required to add a small amount of sugar to your mixture, measure the amount carefully as too much sweetness (like to much salt) can prevent the yeast from working properly. Specially formulated sweet-bread recipes are often heavier in texture than more traditional-style loaves.

Fats

A small amount of fat is added to some breads to improve texture and flavour by slightly enriching the dough, but many plain doughs are made without any fat at all. In very rich mixtures such as brioche (page 102), the fat is added after the dough has been formed. The more fat that is added, the more the fat coats the strands of gluten and slows down fermentation and the dough's rising capacity. Unsalted butter or margarine (unsalted to prevent over-seasoning), lard, white vegetable fat and vegetable oils are all used in bread mixtures. Reduced-fat spreads are less reliable because of their increased water content and are best avoided.

Extras and additions

Once you've got the breadmaking bug, you'll want to start experimenting
by adding other ingredients to your tried-and-tested recipes. There are
plenty of additional items that can be added to doughs to provide health
benefits or to give more flavour, colour and change the texture.

Eggs

The addition of egg will increase the
nutritional content of a loaf as well as
give it more colour and a richer
texture. Always use fresh eggs, free
range or organic for the best flavour
and colour, and use them at room
temperature. Remember that using
egg will increase the liquid volume
of your recipe, so break them into a
jug and beat lightly, then top up
with liquid to the stated amount in
the recipe. Adding egg as well as
the full quantity of liquid will
make the dough too soft and will
make it difficult to produce a good
result when baked.

Dairy products

As well as using milk as the liquid in breadmaking, you can enrich a loaf
further by replacing some of the liquid with natural yoghurt, evaporated
milk, buttermilk, and soft cheese products such as fromage frais, Quark
or cottage cheese. For a very rich texture, you can use small amounts
of full-fat soft cheeses such as mascarpone or cream cheese, and single,
whipping or double cream. The higher the fat content of the dairy produ
you add, the more close-textured and less risen your loaf will be. Added
correctly, small amounts of dairy products will enhance the moisture of
the bread crumb and add a richness of flavour.

Cheese

This is a very popular additional ingredient to savoury and some sweet doughs. Grated cheese can be added at the beginning of the breadmaking, mixed into the flour so it can be thoroughly incorporated to give a rounded savoury flavour. You can also add cheese when you are kneading the bread, which will result in distinct pieces of cheese in your finished loaf. It can also be sprinkled on top to make a cheesy crust. Choose a well-flavoured cheese in small amounts for best results – Parmesan, farmhouse or mature Cheddar, Roquefort or Stilton are all good choices. Remember that many cheeses are quite salty so you may need to reduce the amount in your recipe. Adding too much cheese to your bread will result in a soft dough – remember the cheese will melt and increase the liquid and fat content – so weigh it out accurately and don't be tempted to over-cheese the dough!

Marzipan

This ingredient is worth a mention of its own as it is one of my favourites and you can treat it just like a sweet variety of cheese! Use golden or natural block marzipan depending on your preference. Grate it and mix it into the flour at the beginning so that it melts into the cooked bread or add small pieces during kneading. You can also sprinkle grated or small crumbled pieces on top of your loaf before baking for a sweet, almondy crust. Some festive recipes such as stöllen (page 114) have a layer of marzipan running right through the bread dough. Just like cheese though, adding too much will result in a heavy dough as the marzipan will weigh down the mixture and hinder the rise.

Fibre

Many loaves of bread are a good source of dietary fibre anyway, but this can be enhanced further by adding other ingredients. If you find 100 percent wholemeal bread just a bit too virtuous, you could try adding a source of dietary fibre to your white flour. Extra liquid is usually required when adding more dry ingredients as fibre absorbs more moisture than flour.

Fibre additions

Remember that adding too much bran will inhibit gluten activity so measure accurately:

• Wheat and oat bran are excellent sources of fibre but add no more than 2 tbsp per 225 g (8 oz) flour
• Wheatgerm is a good source of vitamin E as well as adding a delicious mild nutty flavour.
• Rolled oats can be added plain or lightly toasted to a dough to give a more chewy texture and slight nutty flavour. Use the same ratios as for wheat and oat bran.
• Unsweetened muesli containing chopped nuts, vine fruits and cereals add flavour, texture and nutritional quality to your loaf. Use the same ratios as for wheat and oat bran.
• Cooked brown or wild rice are excellent choices for gluten-free breads. Rice will help keep a bread dough moist, and adds fibre, texture and a nutty flavour. Use 50 g (2 oz) cooked rice to 225 g (8 oz) flour.

Nuts and seeds

Small whole or chopped nuts and seeds can be added to the flo
at the beginning of a recipe to add texture and flavour. You
can also replace some of the cereal flour in a recipe with
finely ground nuts – ground almonds, chestnuts, toaste
hazelnuts and unsweetened coconut add flavour and a

delicious richness to a loaf; and are perfect for gluten-free cooking too. Remember that nuts and seeds are rich in oils and adding a groundnut 'flour' to a mixture will increase the fat content and affect the rise of the dough. Replace 4–6 tbsp of the flour in your recipe with finely ground nuts for best results.

Chocolate

Melted chocolate can be mixed into your chosen liquid at the start of the breadmaking process. Alternatively, you can mix cocoa powder into the flour as you would when making a chocolate cake. Small pieces of chocolate or chocolate chips can be added when kneading the dough to give small pockets of molten chocolate when the bread is freshly baked (see page 118).

Great additions

- Grated raw and cooked vegetables
- Soaked and finely chopped dried vegetables (use the soaking liquid in your recipe as well for extra flavour)
- Small dried vine fruits and chopped dried or candied fruit pieces
- Mashed or grated cooked root vegetables such as beetroot, parsnip, carrot or potato
- Tinned and drained or thawed frozen sweetcorn
- Chopped stoned olives
- Mashed ripe banana
- Small fresh berries
- Finely chopped or grated raw apple or pear or stewed or puréed cooked fruit

Fruit and vegetables

There are a host of fruits and vegetables that can be added to breads to add flavour and texture and they can be used in many forms (see box left). The texture of the dough will often become heavier by adding something to it and the extra bulk from the added ingredient will inhibit the rise of the bread. Also be mindful of the extra water content when using fresh fruit and vegetables, which may make the dough more sticky and wet. Try to find a reference recipe to use as a guide (for a recipe, see page 120).

Meat

To make a really savoury bread perfect for a picnic or packed lunch, chop up small pieces of cold cooked meat such as chorizo, salami, smoked bacon or ham and stir into the flour at the beginning of your recipe. Be mindful of the fact that the meat may be adding a certain amount of fat to your recipe, so make suitable adjustments.

Flavourings

There are all sorts of seasonings you can use to perk up your recipe; both dried and fresh herbs are welcome additions as are home ground spices. Dried herbs and ready-ground spices add a more concentrated flavour hit than using freshly chopped herbs or grinding your own spices, so use them more sparingly. One of the most popular flavours is garlic – fresh garlic has anti-fungal properties and can inhibit the function of yeast. Always use fresh garlic sparingly in bread doughs,

and slightly increasing the quantity of yeast can help reduce any possible anti-fungal effects.

Alternatively, try dried garlic products such as powder or flakes or replace the salt in your recipe with garlic-flavoured salt. Try some of the following:

- Dried and freshly chopped herbs such as parsley, chives, rosemary or sage
- Finely chopped fresh or dried chillies or dried onion flakes
- Ground spices or crushed whole spices (toast lightly first for more depth of flavour). cinnamon, cardamon, cumin and fennel are particularly good
- Finely grated citrus rind
- Small pieces of preserved ginger
- Good-quality flavour extracts and essences, such as vanilla, almond or lemon.

Equipment

You don't need much in the way of specialist equipment to make your own bread, but there are a few useful bits and pieces that will help you achieve better results. If you want to experiment beyond the basics, then there is a whole host of (non-essential) breadmaking paraphernalia out there as well as dedicated bakeware for particular kinds and shapes of loaves.

Weighing and measuring

For most baking it is important to be able to weigh and measure your ingredients accurately, and breadmaking is no exception. It is a good idea to invest in a good set of weighing scales if you don't already have them.

You should use a set of weighing scales with a minimum weighing capacity of at least 15 g (½ oz) and these days relatively inexpensive digital scales can achieve that accuracy very easily. You will also need a medium-size glass or plastic measuring jug and a set of measuring spoons. As with all cooking, use one set of measurements throughout the recipe, and don't chop and change between metric and imperial. Unless otherwise stated, all teaspoon and tablespoon measurements are level not heaped.

If you are using fresh and dried yeast you might find thermometer a useful tool for achieving the correct liquid temperature. Once you have made bread a few times you will get a feel for what is correct; using a thermometer is a good fail-safe precaution.

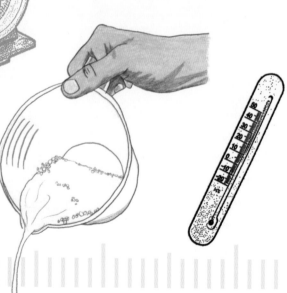

Mixing and rising

You will need some large mixing bowls of glass, china or plastic – these are best since metal can react with yeast – and large bowls will give you plenty of room to mix the dough and allow enough space for the dough to rise.

A wooden spoon and a clean pair of hands are all you need for mixing. A clean tea towel or piece of muslin (cheesecloth) is a good covering for rising dough or you can use a loose covering of oiled clingfilm.

A wooden rolling pin is helpful if you plan to make flatter loaves, but you can also achieve quite a thin dough by pushing and pressing with your hands.

If you plan to make bread using a sourdough starter, it is worth investing in a large glass storage jar with a good sealing lid – a large kilner-type jar used for preserving is a good choice as it has a non-corrosive tight-fitting seal, ideal for long-term storage in the refrigerator.

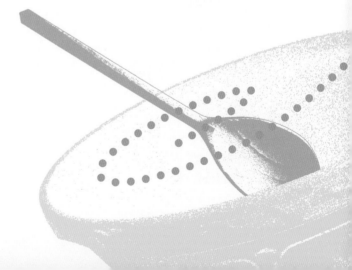

Appliances

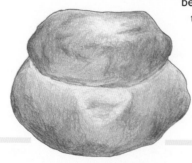

If you have the budget and the kitchen space, you can lighten the worklo
by letting an electrical appliance do the mixing and kneading for you.

Some hand mixers have special dough hooks, and food processo
often have a plastic blade for mixing bread mixtures. A free-
standing heavy-duty mixer is the ultimate in labour-saving
gadgets and will happily churn away your bread dough with
special hook designed for the job, and fully develop the
elasticity of the dough while you get on with something else
Always refer to the manufacturer's instructions for specific
guidelines, settings and fittings for making bread dough. Only us
an appliance if the manufacturer states it is suitable for breadmaki
in order to avoid overheating the appliance or damaging it with prolonge
use. A purist would think that using one of these appliances does not fit
with the whole self-sufficiency ethos, and I agree to a certain extent, as I
haven't included any specific instructions for making dough using a labou
saving machine. However, it's good to know that there is something that
can make life a little easier should you require it.

Breadmakers
This seems like the perfect point to mention the electronic breadmaker,
appliance that will make the whole loaf for you from mixing and proving
baking. Seen as a wonderful invention by many because it 'works while yo
play', making bread in a machine is quite a different technique, and I am n
covering it in this book. If you are curious, it is alwa
best to follow the manufacturer's instructions an
the recipe leaflet that comes with your
particular machine, or refer to a specialist
breadmaker cookery book.

'ins, bakeware and other bits and pieces

Good-quality bakeware is an important factor in helping you achieve perfect loaves. Buy the best that you can afford and they will last you a very long time.

It is worth investing in **heavy-gauge tins** and **trays** since these are less likely to warp in the oven under the higher cooking temperatures required in breadmaking. A basic 900 g (2 lb) and 450 g (1 lb) loaf tin along with a good-quality 18–20 cm (7–8 inch) deep round cake tin and a sturdy baking tray for individual rolls or a free-formed loaf should get you started. Once you have more experience you may want to invest in other shaped tins such as a fluted brioche tin or a perforated baguette tray.

A **pastry brush** is an important piece of kit for glazing your loaves with beaten egg or other finishes before and after baking. Make sure the brush ends are soft so that glazes can be applied easily and softly without damaging the dough.

Once your bread is baked, you need to turn it out onto a **wire rack** to cool. The rack allows air to circulate all round the loaf, cooling it more quickly, helping steam to escape, and crisp up the crust.

Finally, when your loaf is cool and ready to serve, a **wooden board** is the best surface for slicing bread. Keep the board just for bread to avoid transference of flavours and for obvious hygiene reasons. Use a large **serrated-edge knife** for cutting slices of bread.

Basic techniques

It's time to move on to one of the most important parts of the book – how to get started. There are a few techniques involved in making bread, none of which is complicated, but they are vital nonetheless if you want to get a good result. I've broken down the process into ten simple stages described as if you were following a recipe.

Preparing the leaveners – step 1

Breadmaking generally uses some form of leavener to make the dough rise; this is done in various ways but the most common leaveners are yeasts in various forms, and sourdough starters.

Yeasts

All yeast requires some moisture to help it begin to work. Fresh and dried yeasts actually have water added to the yeast, whereas easy-blend yeast is activated by the moisture added to the dough. Water is the most common ingredient with which to start your yeast but you will need to be mindful of the temperature of the water; if using a thermometer, the ideal temperature is 37°C (98.6°F). If you don't have a thermometer, mix two-thirds cold water with one-third boiling water to make a tepid temperature that you can touch comfortably. If the liquid is too hot it will destroy the yeast, too cold and it will not activate it. However, if your kitchen is exceptionally warm, you can use cooler water in order to slow down the rising process.

Fresh yeast Crumble into a glass bowl and add tepid liquid according to your recipe. Using a wooden spoon, mix the yeast until it dissolves and forms a smooth paste. It is then ready to use.

Dried yeast Measure the stated amount of tepid liquid into a glass jug and sprinkle over the dried yeast. Set it aside in a warm place for about 5 minutes, then stir with a wooden spoon to dissolve thoroughly. In this time, the mixture should become frothy, which indicates that the yeast has started to work.

Easy-blend yeast Measure the flour required in the recipe and place in large mixing bowl, then sprinkle the yeast over the flour. Mix it into the flour BEFORE adding the tepid liquid.

Sourdough starter

You need to make some advance preparations if you are planning to use starter to make bread. Depending on the recipe you are following, it can take from 24 hours to several days to prepare and ferment, but the ingredients are always the same: flour, water and yeast. The following is a starter recipe you can use in some of the recipes in this book:

Storing your starter

If you are not using the starter straight away, cover it with clingfilm and store in the refrigerator for up to 2 weeks. Let it stand at room temperature for 30 minutes before using. Once established the starter can be kept indefinitely if stored and used correctly. Every time you use some of the starter, you simply replace the flour and water. If you don't use any starter for two weeks, you will need to replenish it (see below). For long-term use, it is a good idea to store your starter in a large, clean non-corrosive kilner-type jar with a secure rubber seal.

Replenishing a starter

If your recipe uses 300 ml (10 fl oz) starter, you need to replace the amount taken out with 125 g (4½ oz) bread flour and 150 ml (5 fl oz) water. Carefully blend the old and the new ingredients together and leave to ferment as before for 24 hours, then return to the fridge until required again. This should be an ongoing process enabling you to make a sourdough loaf whenever you want.

Making a sourdough starter

- Prepare 25 g (1 oz) fresh yeast or 1 tbsp dried yeast with 200 ml (7 fl oz) tepid water as described above. (If using easy-blend yeast, simply stir 4 tsp into the flour before adding any water, see next step).
- Put 500 g (1 lb 2 oz) white bread flour (or use rice flour for a gluten-free starter) and prepared yeast into a very large, clean glass bowl (the mixture will bubble and rise quite a bit). Gradually stir in a further 400 ml (14 fl oz) tepid water.
- Mix well with a wooden spoon to make a smooth, thick batter. Cover the bowl with a clean tea towel or piece of muslin (cheesecloth).
- Keep the mixture at a coolish room temperature out of direct sunlight, and leave undisturbed for about 3 to 5 days. The batter is ready to use when it begins to froth and has a fresh, pleasant sour aroma. Follow the instructions in your recipe for using the starter.

Mixing the ingredients – step 2

At this stage all your ingredients meet each other for the first time. There will be subtle variations between recipes but in general this is the route to follow:

If using fresh or dried yeast, put the required amount of flour and salt in a large bowl – if making flavoured breads, your recipe may state that other ingredients are added at this stage too. Make a well in the centre using a wooden spoon. If you are using easy-blend yeast, make a well in the centre of your combined dry flour and yeast mixture.

Pour the yeasty liquid in the centre of the well if using and gently mix together with a little of the flour. Some recipes require that the mixture forms a soft paste using just sufficient amounts of flour from the edges of the bowl. The mixture is then covered and left in a warm place for a specified time to expand. This Sponge Method gives a loaf with lighter crumb and less yeasty flavour. After the paste has risen, continue as below.

Gradually pour and mix in the remaining liquid, stirring in all the dry ingredients from the edges of the bowl. As you add liquid the consistency of the mixture changes as it draws together. Don't add all the liquid in one go as it will be difficult to obtain an even blend and you may end up not needing all the amount of liquid.

Only continue to add liquid until the dough is mixed together to form a softish, ball-like mixture in the bowl. If it is still too dry after you have added all the liquid, add a little more. Variations in manufacturing processes and in flour quality can affect the amount of liquid necessary to achieve the desired texture.

neading the dough – step 3

At this stage of breadmaking you establish the basic structure of the mixture. By kneading you distribute the yeast throughout the dough so that it can start to work producing the gases that make an even texture and cause the bread to rise. At the same time, you are helping to form the gluten that creates the framework and holds the risen dough in place during baking.

Very lightly dust a clean, dry work surface with the same type of flour you are using in the recipe.

Turn the prepared, well-mixed contents of your bowl onto the surface and bring the dough together by continually folding the edges into the centre until it becomes smoother and easier to work with – if you find the mixture very sticky, add a little flour but always use extra flour sparingly to avoid making the dough too dry.

Using the heel of one hand, push the dough from the middle, away from you, then roll up the top edge of the dough back towards you. With the other hand, turn the dough slightly, so that you are gradually pushing and rolling the dough round in a circle. Make sure you keep rotating in one direction only to help form an even texture – I usually turn the dough clockwise because I am right-handed, but you can do it however you like!

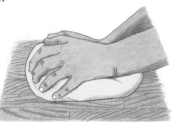

Keep kneading for about 10 minutes or until the dough feels smooth, firm elastic and springy to the touch. Keep pushing the dough from the middle away from you, then rolling up the
top edge of the dough back towards
you. It can be quite difficult to
ascertain that you've kneaded the
dough enough, so try the following
test: take a small piece of the dough
and stretch it so that it is very,
very thin. If the dough is properly
kneaded, it should stretch very
thinly without breaking – as thin
as blown bubble gum. If the dough doesn't stretch easily and tears, then
carry on kneading a bit more. This test is more difficult with wholemeal
and grain doughs because of the fibre in the dough, and in enriched dough
the fats coat the flour and affect its flexibility. However, it is still a reliable
means to see how far you have come in preparing the dough.

When you have achieved the desired
texture, form the dough into a
smooth ball ready for the next stage.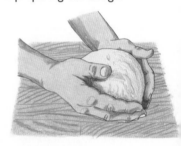

Additions

Towards the end of the kneading process is the perfect time to add flavourings to your bread mixture, including pieces of cheese, chocolate, dried fruits and marzipan. Adding them at this stage will mean they get properly incorporated without being over-processed.

sing and knocking back – step 4

This part of the breadmaking process isn't an exact science since outside factors will affect the rate at which your dough rises. Warmth and increased humidity will speed up the dough rise, but the type of flour and whether you have used a starter can also have an effect. When you have made a few loaves, knowing the rising time of the dough will become second nature, but for the first time it can be difficult to gauge. You should aim for a slow, steady rising process and don't be tempted to speed things up. The test tip will help you decide if your dough is ready for the next stage.

Once your dough has been thoroughly kneaded and shaped into a ball, place it in a lightly floured or oiled glass, china or plastic bowl big enough to allow room for the dough to double in size.

Cover the bowl with a clean tea towel or muslin (cheesecloth) and leave to rise at room temperature out of draughts; a cool temperature is fine, but a very cold room will mean that the yeast will take a long time to get going.

Test tip

Before you leave the dough to rise, press the top of the dough a little with your finger and it should spring back almost immediately. Remember this action as this is a good bench mark indicator for later on when you want to know if your bread has risen enough.

In ideal conditions, the dough should take 1½–2 hours to double in size. Wholemeal flours and enriched doughs take longer. The slower the dough takes to rise, the more flavour and texture the loaf will have.

If you run out of time or your room is very cold, you can put the dough
the refrigerator for at least 8 hours where it will rise slowly and steadily
Cover the bowl with oiled clingfilm – make sure the bowl is big enough
for the dough to expand without being restricted – and then put in the
refrigerator. The dough will then need to stand for about 2 hours at roo
temperature before proceeding to the next stage.

To test that the dough has risen properly, remember the test you carrie
out before you put your dough aside to rise. Now, gently press the dough
again with your finger. If the indent in the dough springs back gradually
then the dough has properly risen; if the indent springs back quickly, the
needs to be left longer. If you've left the dough too long, the indent won
spring back at all and the dough is over-risen, in which case see the
Troubleshooting guide on page 64.

Once the dough has risen to your
satisfaction, push your knuckles
into the dough to deflate it and
turn it out onto a lightly floured
surface; this process is called
knocking back (see right).

Let the dough rest for 5 minutes
on the work surface before you
shape it. Once again, form the
dough into a ball by cupping it in
your hands and gently turning it on
the work surface. As you turn the
dough, gently press your hands
down the sides of the dough to
smooth the sides and then tuck the
edges underneath. Keep turning and
tucking until the dough forms a
smooth ball shape.

haping your loaves – step 5

There are many ways to shape the dough ready for baking, and in the next few points, I will explain some of the basic shapes for loaves and rolls. You will find instructions for shaping specialist doughs in the methods of some of the individual recipes.

Shaping is an important part of breadmaking as it helps the structure and texture of the finished loaf. Sprinkle the work surface lightly with the flour you have used to make the dough. Handle the dough with care – at this point, over-shaping and heavy-handedness will cause the dough to tighten and feel hard (let it rest for a few minutes if this happens and then proceed again gently).

Tin-baked loaf
Keeping the dough in a round shape, flatten it gently with the palm of your hand to remove any large air pockets. Fold one side into the centre and seal it gently, then repeat with the other side so that the two folds overlap in the middle.

Press down gently and turn the dough over so it is seam-side down. Gently roll the dough, keeping an even thickness, until it is 5 cm (2 in) longer than your tin. Carefully lift the dough and fold the ends underneath so it will fit the tin, and lower it into the prepared tin, seam-side down.

Long shaped loaf
Follow the instructions for a tin-baked loaf but roll the dough to fit your prepared baking tray or to the measurements given in your recipe. There is no need to tuck the ends underneath for this loaf, but you may want to press the ends together to seal them neatly. Transfer to the baking tray, seam-side down.

Round loaf

Put the risen dough ball on the work surface and place your hands round the outside. Push your fingers into the base of the dough, tucking the dough into the centre of the ball. Turn the dough in your hands and keep tucking the sides underneath until the dough becomes smooth and rounded. Turn the dough over and pinch the seams together – this will be the bottom of the loaf.

Turn the dough back over and cup it in your hands, rotating and smoothing it until you are satisfied with the shape. Transfer it to your baking tray. Note: this rounded dough can also be cooked in a large round tin if you prefer. The baked loaf will be straight-sided with a large domed top.

Oval loaf

Follow the instructions above to make a round loaf. Once you have formed the dough correctly, gently press either side of the centre with flat, stretched fingers and gently roll the dough backwards and forwards, applying even pressure, until the dough becomes sufficiently tapered at the ends. Transfer to a baking sheet.

Dinner rolls

Roll pieces of dough about the size of a tangerine into small rounds and press down to get rid of any air bubbles. Cup the dough in your hand and roll it on the floured surface until it forms a smooth round roll.

Splits

Form the dough pieces into rounds as above, then gently start rolling the dough from either side of the middle using your fingers. As you roll, the dough will naturally taper at the ends.

Knots, twists and plaits

For **knots**, use pieces of dough about the size of a tangerine, and roll out using the palm of your hand to make a long sausage about 20 cm (8 in) long. Tie into a simple loose knot.

For **twists**, roll the dough into a sausage about 25 cm (10 in) long and fold in half, then simply twist the two pieces together and pinch at the ends to seal.

For **plaits**, roll your dough into a 30 cm (12 in) length, cut into three pieces and plait together (see two illustations below), pinching at the ends to seal.

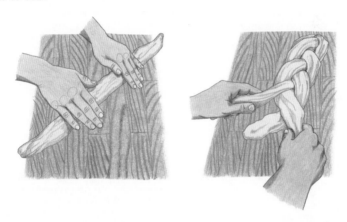

Parker House rolls

Form the dough pieces into rounds as for dinner rolls, then press to form neat circles about 1 cm (½ inch) thick. Brush with beaten egg and fold over, ensuring the top piece of dough overlaps the bottom. Press down lightly on the folded edge.

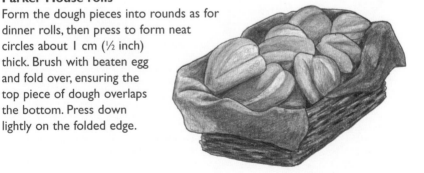

Proving – step 6

Once your loaf or rolls have been shaped and either put in a baking tin or onto a baking tray, the shaped dough needs to rest and rise again before baking. This final rising is referred to as proving and is best done in a warm draught-free place.

Cover the loaf tin or trays of rolls with a sheet of lightly oiled clingfilm – drape it loosely to allow the dough to rise unhindered underneath.

Leave the dough until it has doubled in size, feels spongy to the touch and any indents gradually spring back. If in doubt, it is better to slightly under prove the dough; if it proves for too long, the loaf will collapse in the oven.

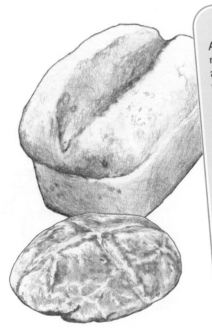

Adding decorative touches

After proving, your bread is now ready for the oven. If you want to add any decorative touches, now is the time to do it – use a sharp knife or a pair of kitchen scissors. For a large loaf, use a small sharp-bladed knife to make a slash down the length of the loaf about 1 cm (½ in) deep – this will encourage an even rising without cracking. Criss-cross cutting is also another way of ensuring an even rise on a large loaf. You can slash the middle of oval-shaped rolls as well.

For baguettes, slash the loaf diagonally as directed in the recipe (see pages 92–93). For rounded rolls, snip the top in a cross using scissors and pull back the points to make an open-cross shape.

pplying glazes and finishes – step 7

Most glazes and toppings are added to the dough once it has proved. You do need to be careful to avoid damaging the surface before baking. There is a wide selection of ingredients you can use to embellish the dough and add extra flavour, colour and texture depending on the desired effect.

lazes

These usually take a liquid form and are brushed onto the surface of your bread before it goes in the oven to be baked, although there are finishes that are added as soon as a loaf comes out of the oven. Here are a few things you might like to try.

Egg wash The most traditional golden-shiny finish for both sweet and savoury breads consists of a beaten egg; simply brush over the dough before baking. For an extra-rich brown glaze, reapply the glaze halfway through baking. For a less golden, but glossy glaze, use beaten egg white only with water. For a rich golden crust, blend 1 egg yolk with 1 tbsp water.

Milk Brush over the dough for a golden crust on sweet and savoury breads.

Melted butter, vegetable margarine and **olive oil** Brush over sweet or savoury loaves to give a soft crust, golden finish and extra-rich flavour.

Dairy- and **egg-free wash** Make a thin smooth paste of soy or corn flour and water, and brush over the surface of the dough. This gives a lightly golden colour and chewy crust to sweet or savoury breads.

Flour dusting Simply dust a little flour over the top of the proved dough before baking – use a small fine sieve for best results. This will give a soft crust to a baked sweet or savoury loaf.

Honey or **maple syrup** For a sticky sweet finish, brush runny honey or maple syrup over bread as soon as it comes out of the oven.

Glacé icing For sweet breads and rolls, sift 115 g (4 oz) icing sugar into bowl and gradually add 3–4 tsp warm water to make a smooth soft icing. Flavour with vanilla or almond extract, or citrus rind for extra flavour, or use freshly squeezed lemon, lime or orange juice instead of water to bind the icing if preferred. Drizzle over bread once the loaf or buns have cooled.

Water Brushing water onto a proved loaf or spraying with a light mister just before baking will give a crisp, golden crust. This technique is used in preparing French baguettes (see page 92).

Applying toppings

As well as brushing the dough with a glaze, you may want to add a topping. The glaze will act as an adhesive to enable you to keep the topping in place. Here are some embellishments you may like to try:

• Small seeds; finely chopped or flaked nuts; rolled oats; bran flakes; cracked wheat; cornmeal
• Grated cheese; finely shredded cooked onion
• Coarse salt; freshly ground black pepper
• Lightly cracked spice seeds such as fennel, caraway, cumin and coriander
• A little chilli powder, plain or smoked paprika, or tiny sprigs of fresh herbs.

For sweet breads try:
• Poppy seeds; rolled oats
• Coarse sugar such as Demerara or granulated; crushed sugar lumps
• Ground spices such as cinnamon, ginger, allspice and finely crushed cardamom seeds
• Baked sweet breads can also be dusted with icing sugar just before serving.

aking – step 8

Baking is the next important step in breadmaking. Always preheat the oven to the temperature given in the particular recipe, although most breads cook in a hot oven at about 220°C (420°F/gas mark 7). If you have a fan oven, refer to the manufacturer's guidelines as you may need to adjust the temperature. In an ideal world, bread requires an even temperature but all ovens cook differently and temperatures may vary so if in any doubt, use an oven thermometer to check yours. If your oven has a 'hot spot', turn your bread round halfway through the cooking time.

Place your bread on the middle shelf of the oven. Cooking times vary depending on the recipe and the size of your loaf. Some recipes call for extra moisture or steam during baking and this can be achieved by placing a tray of water in the bottom of the oven.

When is it done?

Unlike a cooked cake mixture, there is a firm crust to contend with on a loaf of bread, so it is impossible to see whether the dough is properly cooked on the inside. However, a perfectly cooked loaf will be risen, have a golden brown crust and the texture should feel firm but not hard. Cover your hand with a clean oven cloth and carefully turn the bread out. Tap the underside of the loaf gently with your fingers; it will sound hollow when it is properly cooked.

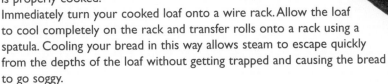

Immediately turn your cooked loaf onto a wire rack. Allow the loaf to cool completely on the rack and transfer rolls onto a rack using a spatula. Cooling your bread in this way allows steam to escape quickly from the depths of the loaf without getting trapped and causing the bread to go soggy.

The perfect slice – step 9

For maximum freshness, always cut bread just before serving as it dries out quickly and becomes stale. Bread doesn't have to be completely coo before you cut it, but if too hot, the knife will drag the crumbs together and make the texture doughy; nor will you benefit from the flavour if the bread is too hot when you eat it. Bread of all types is traditionally serve in wicker or cane ware – this natural fibre helps keep the bread fresh, ar will tolerate warmth.

To cut the perfect slice, sit the loaf on a clean wooden board (used only for bread) and cut with a sharp, serrated bread-knife. Use a steady sawing action across the top of the crust and continue straight down the loaf, sawing all the tim to prevent spoiling the crumb – if you press dow on a loaf you will risk squishing the crumbs together, causing a doughy texture.

Reheating

If you've baked bread earlier in the day and want to serve it warm for your guests or family, try th very easy and economical way I have discovered that avoids puttir on the conventional oven. Simply put cooked rolls in a slow cooker dish, cover with the lid, switch onto the hi setting and leave for about 25 minutes to warm through.

To use more conventional means, arrange your bread on a baking tray, spray lightly with water and place uncovered in a preheated oven at abou 200°C (400°F/gas mark 6). Crusty loaves will take about 5 minutes to warm and crisp, rolls need only 2–3 minutes. Pitta and naan breads can b reheated by placing under a hot grill for 1–2 minutes on each side – spra them lightly with water too before heating.

oring and freezing – step 10

How long bread stays fresh depends on several factors. Some recipes will state that a certain loaf is best eaten on the day of baking – these tend to be small or thin, plainer breads, for example, white bread rolls, pitta bread and baguettes. Larger, thicker loaves will usually last a few days if stored correctly; loaves enriched with fat or oil are usually good keepers, as are the more rustic breads made with a starter. Gluten-free and yeast-free breads tend to dry out quite quickly once a slice has been taken off. Below are a few tips to help you store your bread.

Bread must be completely cold before storing – any warmth will speed up mould growth or cause the bread to go stale more quickly.

It sounds obvious, but keep bread at room temperature, away from direct sunlight in a cool and dry place in order to maintain freshness.

I always keep the crusty end of the loaf after I've cut it. I then use this as a natural seal for the end of the loaf.

Alternatively, you could wrap the end in clingfilm or aluminium foil but make sure you only cover the end; avoid wrapping the whole loaf as this will make it 'sweat' and lose its crustiness and texture. If you have a clean paper bag, you could wrap this round the bread.

Bread needs to 'breathe' for better keeping. You will find cloth bags (plast bags are not suitable) specifically designed for wrapping round a loaf, but you could try a clean tea towel or piece of muslin (cheesecloth) – a note from personal experience, avoid using a tea towel that has been freshly washed in particularly fragrant washing powder, otherwise you will end u with very strange-tasting bread!

You may prefer to put your wrapped bread away from the work surface; an earthenware crock, wooden, wicker or metal bread bin are suitable, b make sure they don't seal completely tight – air needs to circulate. You ca use a plastic container, but make some holes in the top and sides.

Avoid putting bread in the refrigerator as this makes the bread dehydrate quickly and become stale. It is also likely to absorb aromas from other foods and become tainted.

Freezing bread

For long-term storage, freezing is the obvious solution. You can freeze baked bread as well as uncooked bread dough.

Freezing baked bread

After thoroughly cooling your loaf, either slice it beforehand for convenience or leave it whole. For freezing, bread does need to be well sealed, so wrap in heavy-duty aluminium foil and then either in clingfilm or a large freezer bag. Seal well and keep for up to three months. Rolls and thin breads as well as gluten-free and non-yeasted breads are best frozen as soon as they are cool on the day of baking; they can be wrapped and frozen as for larger loaves. Remember to date and label your breads.

Freezing dough

Once the dough is mixed and kneaded, form it into a neat ball shape. Oil the inside of a clean freezer bag and put the dough inside. Expel all the air, leaving a little room for the dough to expand slightly as it freezes (it will take a while for the yeast to become inactive in the freezer), then seal the bag. Date and label the bag and freeze for up to three months.

Defrosting bread

Cooked bread is best defrosted slowly. I haven't mastered the art of the 'quick defrost' in the microwave oven; it's always been a bit hit-and-miss and I only do it if I'm desperate. I can't recommend a quick way, just the way you should do it! Keep your frozen bread in the freezer wrappings and let it stand at room temperature for about 3 hours, or leave in the refrigerator for up to 10 hours, until it has thawed. When thawed in this way it will be difficult to distinguish it from freshly baked and it should retain good moistness without having dried out. If you want to crisp up the crust, place the thawed loaf in a low or warm oven for 5–10 minutes – no longer, otherwise you will have hot bread! Bread can only be reheated once to crisp it up, after which time it will simply dry out and become stale.

Defrosting bread dough

Carefully remove the dough from the freezer and place in a large oiled glass, china or plastic bowl in the refrigerator – the bowl needs to be big enough to allow sufficient room for the dough to rise. Cover with clingfilm and leave for up to 24 hours or until doubled in size. Remove from the refrigerator, discard the clingfilm and stand the dough at room temperature for 2 hours to thoroughly take the chill off, then you can shape, prove and bake your dough as described previously.

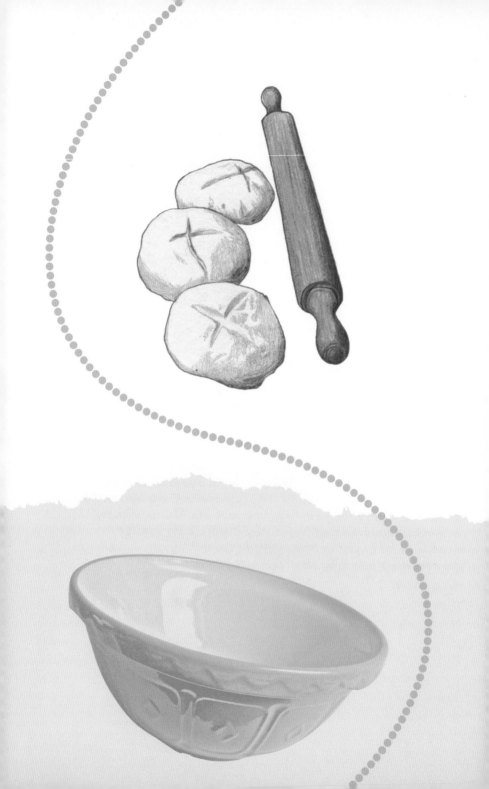

Trouble-
shooting

Sometimes, even when you think you've done everything right, you will experience problems with your baking. It will rarely be the fault of the ingredients you are using, and the most common cause is often lack of preparation of the dough before baking or a fault with the recipe you are following. Always follow recipes from a reliable source and then refer to the information overleaf for solutions to some of the most common problems that you might encounter.

Pre-baking dough problems

There are a number of problems that can occur with your dough at the mixing and rising stages.

Dry dough 1

When first mixing the yeasty liquid into the flour and gradually adding the remaining liquid, you may end up with a crumbly mixture. This is because is virtually impossible to state the exact quantity of liquid required to make a perfectly combined mixture – different flours absorb water at different rates. Simply add more liquid, 1 tsp at a time, mixing it in betwe additions until you have achieved the right consistency.

Dry dough 2

When you come to knead the dough you may find it too stiff and hard to manipulate. Use a water spray add liquid in very small amounts so that the dough absorbs the extra moisture without becoming stic You can also achieve this by wetting your hands w water and using wetted hands to knead the dough Keep wetting them until you have achieved dough the right texture.

Wet dough

If you turn your dough onto the work surface and it seems excessively wet and the dough sticks to your fingers as you work it, dust the dough lightly with the flour used in your recipe and keep kneading in sufficient extra flour in small dustings, until it feels smooth and comes away from your fingers as you knead.

Dough doesn't rise

There could be a number of reasons why your dough hasn't risen.

• The yeast may not be as fresh as you thought – check the expiry date and how it has been stored; if this is the cause, discard the mixture and start a fresh batch.

• The liquid used was either too hot or too cold – the yeast has either been destroyed or not given the right conditions to get it going. If you got the liquid temperature wrong, it is better to start again (see page 46 for how to achieve the right temperature).

• The dough is too dry or stiff – lack of moisture will mean the yeast doesn't work properly, and the gluten doesn't develop in the kneading process (see above).

• If after the rising period, the dough hasn't risen, conditions may be too cold – put the mixture somewhere warmer and see if this sets off the rise. The same can also apply to shaped dough during the proving period.

• Too much salt added to the mixture will inhibit the yeast from working. Measure salt carefully.

Dough has over-risen

• When the dough is very puffed up and the finger test on the risen dough makes an imprint that doesn't spring back, the dough will usually deflate and there will be a strong smell of fermenting yeast. You can try to reclaim the dough by kneading it very briefly, shaping the dough and leaving it for a short proving period before baking. Make sure you leave the dough to rise in a cool temperature for a slow, steady rise – too warm and the yeast will set to work too quickly and not achieve the correct result.

• Another factor to consider if your dough has over-risen is the use of salt. Perhaps you forgot to add any? Salt controls yeast activity and acts a 'brake'; if you haven't added any, there will be a chance that the yeast h become over-active and the dough will expand more than it should. Tast little piece of the dough if you are unsure.

Shaped bread is over-proved

This happens when you leave your shaped bread too long on its second rise before baking. Either the loaf has risen too much in its tin or free-standing loaves or rolls will look puffy and misshapen. If you bake the bread in this state it will more than likely collapse in the oven. Y can try and reclaim the dough in the same way as you would dough that has over-risen (see page 67) but this time only le it to prove for a very short time – just until you can see it starting to rise again. Then bake as directed.

st-baking problems

Sometimes the results that come out of the oven are not what you expect. There are a number of things that can go wrong:

Lack of rise
• Sometimes a loaf will fail to rise in the oven during the baking time; in which case refer to information given for Dry Dough (see page 66).

• Insufficient kneading and lack of gluten development.

• Insufficient rising time – the yeast hasn't had a chance to develop properly (see test on page 51).

Bread has collapsed
• The loaf collapses during the initial cooking period because the extra heat from the oven has caused the dough to over-prove. (See page 68 on Over-proved bread.)

• Too much dough for the tin. Make sure you use the correct amount of dough for your tin. At the extreme, bread dough will run down the side of the tin and the loaf will not form a domed top.

Uneven shape
Either the tin is the wrong size or the dough hasn't been kneaded properly. Always use the size of tin stated in the recipe. Make sure you knead the bread dough thoroughly as directed on pages 49–50 in order to allow the gluten to form a proper structure in the dough. Take care to seal ends of loaves for free-form shapes in order to achieve a neat finish.

Cracked top

Too much flour may have been used during shaping, causing the dough to dry out on top; always use the minimum amount of flour when kneading and preparing the dough. Also, make sure you follow the directions on page 53 for shaping the dough in order to make a smooth, crease-free ba of dough from which to shape your rolls or loaf.

Cracked sides

Insufficient proving can cause this to happen – when the bread goes into the oven it gets a sudden burst of heat and causes the yeast to put on a real spurt of action that makes the structure split. Follow the test on pag 51 for judging the correct amount of time to prove your dough.

Soggy crust

This occurs when the bread has been allowed to cool in the tin. Steam gets trapped and goes back into the loaf as moisture, causing the crust to become soft. Always turn your loaves and rolls out onto a wire rack as soon as they are baked.

Baked crust separates from bread

When you cut into your bread for the first time, yo may encounter a pocket of air running down the lengt of the loaf between the crust and the rest of the bread. This is usually caused when the shaped bread has been left a bit too long to prove in too-dry conditions. This will cause the outside of the loaf to form a crusty edge. The weaker, over-risen dough inside will begin to collapse back away from it because the yea has become exhausted. When the bread is baked in this condition, the to crust forms a thicker crusty edge than normal because it has set in place and the dough underneath is not able to rise up sufficiently to reach it, s an air pocket forms between the rest of the dough and the crust. Prove your bread in the right conditions and follow the instructions on page 56

Crust is pale
In order to obtain a well-formed crust on a loaf make sure your
oven is hot enough – if in doubt check with a special oven
thermometer placed inside the oven. Other factors that
inhibit the formation of the crust can be insufficient
sugar in the dough, lack of moisture, and over-proving
in a warm place mentioned in the previous problem. If
you are concerned about the dough drying out
during rising or proving, cover with a clean, damp tea
towel to keep the conditions moist. You can then
spray the towel lightly with water if necessary.

Crust is too dark
Your oven may be too hot or you may have cooked the bread for too
long – if in doubt, check with a special oven thermometer placed inside
the oven. You can shield a loaf that's browning too quickly with aluminium
foil. It is important to bake bread long enough, otherwise the middle will
be doughy and indigestible. If your bread is an enriched dough, take care to
measure the sugar correctly as an excess can cause the crust to darken
quickly before the rest of the bread is thoroughly cooked.

Crust is too thick
This problem is often found in a loaf where a crust has separated from
the rest of the bread and the final rise has been overdone. But it can also
occur in an enriched bread dough if there isn't sufficient sugar to brown
off a top crust.

White floury patches present in cooked loaf
This may happen when you use too much extra flour during kneading or
shaping. The flour gets into the dough but doesn't get thoroughly mixed in,
so it just sits in the dough as raw flour. Try to refrain from adding sprinkles
of flour during the last stages of kneading, and if you do, keep it as light as
possible – use a small fine sieve for minimal dusting.

Bread texture problems

Occasionally, the loaf that comes out of the oven may look fine from the outside and doesn't reveal its imperfections until you cut into it. Here are some common problems:

Sour flavour and smell
• Most commonly this will occur if the dough has been over-risen or has risen too quickly in too high a temperature; you will probably detect an over-yeasty smell too (see page 67).

• If you don't cook your bread for long enough, the yeast will not be destroyed by sufficient heat, and the aroma and flavour will linger in th bread – it will also be doughy in texture.

> **Rising tip**
>
> Stop the rising process when the dough has doubled in size, and carry out the test on top of the dough with your finger (see page 51).

Heavy and claggy
• The bread has been baked at too high a temperature if the texture is heavy and claggy. If in doubt, use an oven thermometer. If the crust browns too early, the loaf can't expand to its maximum volume. This means the inner texture of the bread doesn't form correctly and remains close-crumbed and under-risen.

• Insufficient cooking time. Just because the outside looks done, if the baking is actually incomplete, the inner crumb will be gummy and lacking in flavour. Remember that undercooked bread is indigestible. See page 59 for how to check if bread is cooked properly.

Too crumbly and dry

If the texture of the bread is too crumbly and dry it could be that you've used a poor-grade flour that doesn't contain enough gluten. Always use good-quality fresh flour from good sources for best results .

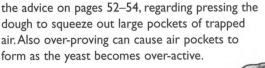

Coarse texture, dark colour

This problem is caused by not using the correct flour as stated in the recipe. For best results, select flour carefully and buy the best quality you can afford from a source with a good turnover.

Large air holes

While you want your bread to have some holes, large pockets of air are unsatisfactory unless symptomatic of a recipe (e.g. ciabatta). Usually this is caused by poor kneading so that the yeast is badly distributed in the dough. When you are shaping the dough, make sure you follow the advice on pages 52–54, regarding pressing the dough to squeeze out large pockets of trapped air. Also over-proving can cause air pockets to form as the yeast becomes over-active.

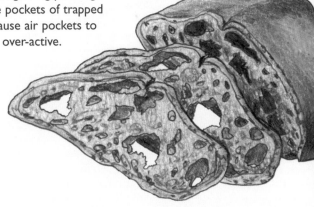

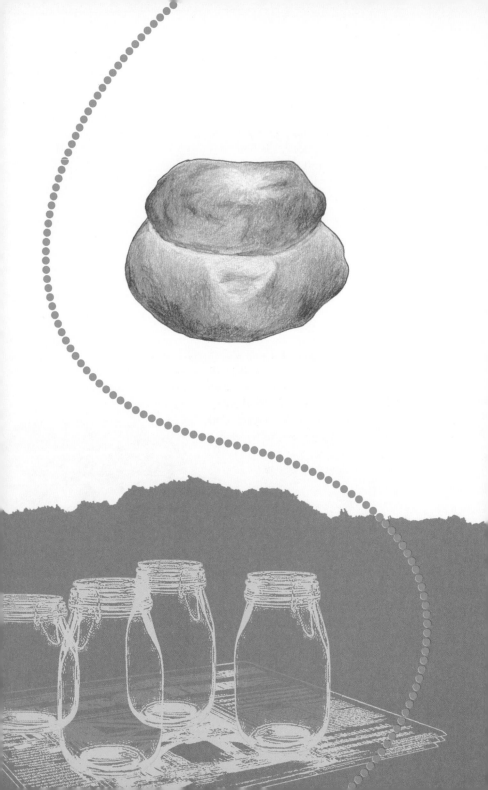

Bread recipes

Nothing can compare to the lovely aroma of freshly baked bread wafting from your kitchen. In the following pages you will find recipes for delicious breads from around the world, but there are also some basic recipes to start you off. Try a classic white loaf before you launch into the exciting world of sourdough starters and French baguettes, crusty rolls and gluten-free loaves.

Basic white bread

This is a good recipe to get you started – from this simple loaf you will be able to make many variations. I tend to use fresh yeast but you can also use dried and easy-blend yeasts.

Makes one 850 g (1 lb 14 oz) tin loaf

20 g (¾ oz) fresh yeast or 2½ tsp dried yeast or 1½ tsp easy-blend yeast

375 ml (13 fl oz) tepid water

550 g (1 lb 4 oz) very strong white bread flour, plus extra for dusting

1¾ tsp salt

Crumble the fresh yeast into a small glass bowl and add 100 ml (3½ fl oz) of the tepid water. Using a wooden spoon, mix the yeast until it dissolves and forms a smooth paste. If using dried yeast, sprinkle yeast over the same amount of tepid water and proceed as for fresh yeast (also see page 46 in Techniques). If using easy-blend yeast, simply mix with your flour before adding any liquid.

Mix the flour and salt in a large mixing bowl and make a well in the centre. Pour the yeasty liquid in the centre of the well and gently mix together using a wooden spoon with a little of the flour.

Gradually pour and mix in the remaining water, carefully stirring in the dry ingredients from the edges of the flour well to form a softish ball-like mixture in the middle.

Turn the dough onto a lightly floured work surface and knead until smooth and elastic, about 10 minutes.

Put the dough in a large, lightly floured glass, china or plastic bowl. Cover with a clean tea towel or muslin (cheesecloth) and leave to rise at a coolish room temperature out of draughts for 1½–2 hours until doubled in size.

Once it has risen satisfactorily, knock back by pushing your knuckles into the dough to deflate it and turn it out onto a lightly floured surface. Form the dough into a ball and let it rest for 5 minutes on the work surface before you shape it.

Grease a 900 g (2 lb) loaf tin. Shape the dough to fit the tin and place it, seam-side down, in the tin. Cover loosely with oiled clingfilm and set aside to prove in a warm place until doubled in size.

Meanwhile, preheat the oven to 220°C (425°F/gas mark 7). Remove the covering from the loaf and using a sharp knife, cut a slash down the centre of the loaf about 1 cm (½ in) deep. Dust lightly with a little flour and bake in the centre of the oven for about 30 minutes. Reduce the temperature to 190°C (375°F/gas mark 5) and bake for a further 15 minutes until golden brown and hollow-sounding when tapped underneath. Turn out onto a wire rack to cool.

White loaf variations

- **For a crusty finish**
Brush the loaf with beaten egg just before baking.
- **For a round tin loaf**
Fit this quantity of dough into a 6 cm (2½ in) deep × 18 cm (7 in) diameter tin. Bake as for a white loaf.
- **For a free-form loaf**
Follow instructions for shaping and baking on pages 53–58 and bake as for a white loaf.
- **To make bread rolls**
Divide the dough into eight equal portions and shape as directed on page 54. Place on a large lightly floured baking tray, cover loosely and leave to prove until doubled in size. Bake in a preheated oven as for a white loaf for about 20 minutes. Transfer to a wire rack to cool.

Free-form white loaf

This variation uses standard plain flour mixed with white bread flour in order to give a softer texture. This dough works best with fresh or standard dried yeast and it's free-form, so no tins required!

Makes one 900 g (2 lb) loaf, roughly 23 cm (9 in) in diameter

25 g (1 oz) fresh yeast or
1 tbsp dried yeast

375 ml (13 fl oz) tepid water

350 g (12 oz) white bread flour

250 g (9 oz) standard white plain flour

2 tsp salt

1 tbsp caster sugar

1 tbsp vegetable oil

Crumble the fresh yeast into a small glass bowl and add 150 ml (5 fl oz) of the tepid water. Using a wooden spoon, mix the yeast until it dissolves and forms a smooth paste. If using dried yeast, sprinkle yeast over the same amount of tepid water and proceed as for fresh yeast (see also page 46 in Techniques).

Mix the flours, salt and sugar in a large mixing bowl and make a well in the centre. Pour the yeasty liquid in the centre of the well of dried ingredients and gently mix together using a wooden spoon with a little of the flour. Stir in the oil.

Gradually pour and mix in the remaining water, carefully stirring in the dry ingredients from the edges of the flour well to form a softish, ball-like mixture in the middle. Turn the dough onto a lightly floured work surface and knead until smooth and elastic, about 10 minutes.

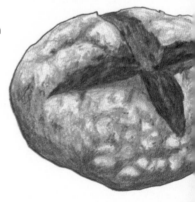

Once the dough has been kneaded to your satisfaction, put the dough in a large, lightly floured glass, china or plastic bowl. Cover with a clean tea towel or muslin (cheesecloth) and leave to rise at a coolish room temperature out of draughts for 1½–2 hours until doubled in size.

Once risen, knock back the dough and turn out onto a lightly floured surface. Form the dough into a ball and let it rest for 5 minutes before you shape it into a round as described on page 54.

Carefully transfer the dough to a large lightly floured baking tray, seam-side down, cover loosely with oiled clingfilm and set aside to prove in a warm place until doubled in size.

Meanwhile, preheat the oven to 220°C (425°F/gas mark 7). Using a sharp knife, carefully cut a cross pattern over the top of the loaf about 1 cm (½ in) deep. Brush with cold water and bake in the centre of the oven for about 30 minutes, until golden brown and hollow-sounding when tapped underneath. Transfer to a wire rack to cool.

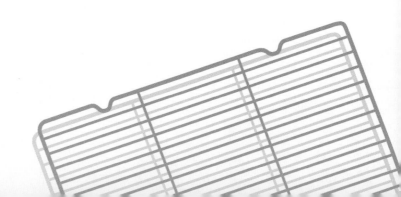

Wholemeal loaf

I do like to eat healthily, but I have always struggled with very fibrous bread. T
is my way of making a wholesome loaf that still feels a bit naughty too!

Makes one 675 g (1½ lb) round tin loaf

15 g (½ oz) fresh yeast or 2 tsp dried
yeast or 1¼ tsp easy-blend yeast

275 ml (9½ fl oz) tepid water

250 g (9 oz) wholemeal bread flour,
plus extra for dusting

200 g (7 oz) white bread flour

1½ tsp salt

1 tbsp light brown sugar

Crumble the fresh yeast into a sma
glass bowl and add to it 100 ml
(3½ fl oz) of the tepid water.
Using a wooden spoon, mix the
yeast until it dissolves and form
a smooth paste. If using dried
yeast, sprinkle yeast over the sa
amount of tepid water and proce
as for fresh yeast (see also page 4
in Techniques). If using easy-blend
yeast, simply mix yeast with flour
before adding any liquid.

Mix the flours, salt and sugar in a
large mixing bowl and make a well
in the centre. Pour the yeasty liquid
into the centre of the well, and gently
mix together with only a little of the flour to form a smooth paste. Cov
with a clean tea towel and leave at room temperature for 20 minutes ur
the paste forms a 'sponge' and is frothy and bubbling.

Gradually pour and mix in
the remaining water,
carefully stirring in the
rest of the ingredients
from the edges of the
flour well to form a
softish, ball-like mixture in the
middle of the bowl.

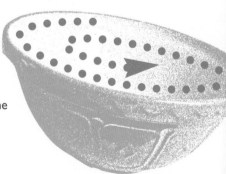

Turn the dough onto a lightly floured work surface and knead until smooth and elastic, about 10 minutes.

Put the dough in a lightly floured bowl big enough to allow the dough to double in size. Cover the bowl with a clean tea towel or muslin (cheesecloth) and leave to rise at a coolish room temperature out of draughts for 1½–2 hours until doubled in size.

Once it has risen satisfactorily, knock back and turn it out onto a lightly floured surface. Form the dough into a ball and let it rest for 5 minutes before you shape it.

Grease and line a 6 cm (2½ in) deep x 18 cm (6 in) diameter tin. Shape the dough to fit the tin and place it in, seam-side down. Cover loosely and set aside to prove in a warm place until doubled in size.

Meanwhile, preheat the oven to 220°C (425°F/gas mark 7). Using a sharp knife, cut a cross pattern in the top of the loaf about 1 cm (½ in) deep. Dust lightly with flour and bake in the centre of the oven for about 30 minutes, until golden brown and hollow-sounding when tapped underneath. Turn out onto a wire rack to cool.

Wholemeal variations

- **Wholemeal rolls**
Use this dough to make six large rolls as described on page 54.
- **Less or more wholemeal**
Use half wholemeal to half white bread flour for a lighter loaf, and for a very wheaty loaf use all wholemeal bread flour. You may have to use slightly more water and knead for a little longer, however.

Granary flowerpot bread

I love the sweet, malty flavour of granary bread. It is best to buy new terracotta pots and keep them for baking purposes only.

Makes six 115 g (4 oz) pot loaves

450 g (1 lb) granary bread flour

1½ tsp salt

1¼ tsp easy-blend yeast

275 ml (9½ fl oz) tepid water

1 egg, beaten, to glaze

Grease and flour or line six 8 cm (3¼ in) diameter and 9 cm (3½ in) deep, clean terracotta flowerpots. In a large bowl, mix the flour and salt. Stir in the easy-blend yeast completely before making a well in the centre.

Gradually pour and mix in the water using a wooden spoon, stirring in the dry ingredients from the edges of the flour well to form a softish, ball-like mixture in the middle. Turn the dough onto a lightly floured work surface and knead until smooth and elastic, about 10 minutes.

Put the dough in a lightly floured glass, china or plastic bowl, big enough to allow the dough to double in size. Cover the bowl with a clean tea towel or muslin (cheesecloth) and leave to rise at a coolish room temperature out of draughts for 1½–2 hours until doubled in size.

Once it has risen satisfactorily, knock back and turn it out on to a lightly floured surface. Form the dough into a ball and let it rest for 5 minutes before you shape it into a round as described on page 53.

Divide the dough into six equal pieces. Form into rounds as described for round rolls on page 54. Place one ball in each pot, seam-side down, to come about halfway up the inside of the pot. Arrange the pots on a large baking sheet, cover loosely with oiled clingfilm and set aside to prove in a warm place until doubled in size.

Meanwhile, preheat the oven to 220°C (425°F/gas mark 7). Brush with beaten egg and bake in the centre of the oven for about 25 minutes until richly golden, risen to the top of the pots and hollow-sounding when tapped underneath. Turn out onto a wire rack to cool; you may need to loosen the loaves from the pots by running a round-bladed knife around the edge of each.

Granary variations

• **Granary rolls**
Use this dough to make six large rolls as described on page 54.

• **For a round tin loaf**
Grease and line a 6 cm (2½ in) deep x 18 cm (7 in) diameter tin, follow the recipe above but shape the dough to fit the tin. Prove and glaze as above, then bake in the oven for about 30 minutes.

• **Seedy loaf**
Granary flour makes an excellent base for a multigrain-and-seed loaf. Replace half the granary flour with wholemeal bread flour and add 1 tbsp poppy seeds, 1 tbsp linseeds (flax seeds) plus 15 g (½ oz) each crushed pumpkin and sunflower seeds. Sprinkle the top of the loaf with extra seeds before baking as well if liked. Bake as for the tin loaf above.

Poppy seed plait

This dough is made using milk as the liquid and is therefore known as a milk loaf. The crumb is finer and the crust soft and glossy.

Makes one 30 cm (12 in) long plaited loaf

15 g (½ oz) fresh yeast or 2 tsp dried yeast or 1½ tsp easy-blend yeast

250 ml (9 fl oz) tepid semi-skimmed milk

450 g (1 lb) white bread flour

1½ tsp salt

1½ tsp caster sugar

1 egg, beaten, to glaze

1 tbsp poppy seeds

Crumble yeast into a small glass bowl and add 100 ml (3½ fl oz) of the tepid milk. Using a wooden spoon mix the yeast until it dissolves and forms a smooth paste. If using dried yeast, sprinkle yeast over the same amount of tepid milk and proceed for fresh yeast (also see page 46 in Techniques). If using easy-blend yeast simply mix with your flour before adding any liquid.

Mix the flour, salt and sugar in a large mixing bowl and make a well in the centre. Pour the yeasty milk in the centre of the well and using a wooden spoon, gently mix together with a little of the flour.

Gradually pour and mix in the remaining milk, carefully stirring in all the dry ingredients from the edges of the flour well to form a softish, ball-like mixture in the middle. Turn the dough onto a lightly floured work surface and knead until smooth and elastic, about 10 minutes.

Put the dough in a lightly floured glass, china or plastic bowl, big enough to allow room for the dough to double in size. Cover the bowl with a clean tea towel or muslin (cheesecloth) and leave to rise at a coolish room temperature out of draughts for 1½–2 hours until doubled in size.

Once it has risen satisfactorily, knock back and turn it out onto a lightly floured surface. Form the dough into a ball and let it rest for 5 minutes before you shape it.

Divide the dough into three equal portions and roll each into a thick sausage about 30 cm (12 in) long. Line up the lengths of dough running towards you. Starting with the left piece, fold it over the centre piece, then fold the right piece over the piece in the centre. Continue plaiting, always folding the outside pieces alternately into the middle until you reach the end. Press the pieces together at both ends and tuck the ends underneath (see page 55 in Techniques for illustrations). Carefully transfer to a large lightly floured baking sheet, seam-side down, cover and set aside to prove in a warm place until doubled in size.

Meanwhile, preheat the oven to 200°C (400°F/gas mark 6). Brush all over with beaten egg. Sprinkle with poppy seeds and bake in the centre of the oven for about 30 minutes, until glossy golden brown and hollow-sounding when tapped underneath. Transfer to a wire rack to cool.

Poppy seed variations

- **For a tin loaf**
Shape the mixture as described on page 53, tuck the ends under to fit the length of a lightly greased 900 g (2 lb) loaf tin, then carefully lower into the tin, seam-side down. Prove, glaze, seed and bake as above.
- **Shaping a cottage loaf**
(See illustration left) Divide the dough into two-thirds and a third. Shape each piece into a round loaf as described on page 54, then flatten slightly. Place the smaller round directly on top of the larger one, and seal them together by pushing two fingers down through the middle of the top loaf. Carefully transfer to a lightly floured baking tray. Prove, glaze, seed and bake as the plait above.

Spelt bloomer

I was introduced to spelt flour several years ago after a visit to a nutritionist due to a poor state of health. To my delight, I was able to enjoy bread again in moderation without the side-effects I'd been suffering.

Makes one 700 g (1 lb 9 oz) loaf

15 g (½ oz) fresh yeast or 2 tsp dried yeast or 1½ tsp easy-blend yeast

275 ml (9½ fl oz) tepid water

1 tbsp heather honey or other strong-flavoured honey

450 g (1 lb) spelt flour

1½ tsp salt

1 tbsp olive oil

Crumble the fresh yeast into a small glass bowl and add 100 ml (3½ fl oz) of the tepid water. Using a wooden spoon, mix the yeast until it dissolves and forms a smooth paste. If using dried yeast, sprinkle yeast over the same amount of tepid water and proceed as for fresh yeast (also see page 46 in Techniques). If using easy-blend yeast, simply mix with your flour before adding any liquid. Dissolve the honey in the remaining water.

Mix the flour and salt in a large mixing bowl and make a well in the centre. Pour the honey and yeasty water in the centre of the well, add the oil and using a wooden spoon, gently mix together with a little of the flour from the edges of the flour well.

Gradually pour and mix in the remaining honey water, carefully stirring in the dry ingredients from the edges of the flour well to form a softish, ball-like mixture in the middle. Turn the dough onto a lightly floured work surface and knead until smooth and elastic, about 10 minutes.

Put the dough in a lightly floured glass, china or plastic bowl, big enough to allow room for the dough to double in size. Cover the bowl and leave to rise at a coolish room temperature out of draughts for 1½–2 hours until doubled in size.

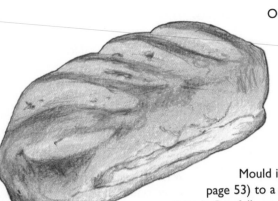

Once the dough has risen satisfactorily, knock back and turn it out onto a lightly floured surface. Form the dough into a ball and let it rest for about 5 minutes before you shape it.

Mould into a long shape (see page 53) to a length of about 25 cm (10 in). Carefully transfer to a large lightly floured baking tray, seam-side down, cover and set aside to prove in a warm place until doubled in size.

Meanwhile, preheat the oven to 200°C (400°F/gas mark 6). Using a sharp knife, cut diagonal slashes about 1 cm (½ in) deep, down the length of the dough. Lightly dust with flour and bake in the centre of the oven for about 35 minutes until lightly golden and hollow-sounding when tapped underneath. Transfer to a wire rack to cool.

Spelt bloomer variations

• **For a tin loaf**
Shape the mixture as described on page 53, but tuck the ends under and place in a lightly greased 900 g (2 lb) loaf tin, seam-side down. Prove, glaze, seed and bake as for the spelt bloomer above.

• **Spelt rolls**
This recipe will make eight rolls. Divide the dough into eight pieces and shape rolls as described on page 54. Bake at 200°C (400°F/gas mark 6) for about 25 minutes.

Gluten-free buckwheat loaves

You can now buy ready-prepared gluten-free bread flour and follow the recipe given on the packet, but this recipe calls for one of my favourite blends of gluten-free flours. It works best using easy-blend yeast.

Makes two 450 g (1 lb) loaves

250 g (9 oz) buckwheat flour

250 g (9 oz) brown rice flour

1½ tsp salt

1 tbsp light brown sugar

2 tsp xanthan gum

2 tsp easy-blend yeast

450 ml (16 fl oz) tepid water

3 tbsp cold-pressed rapeseed oil or other vegetable oil

Grease two 450 g (1 lb) loaf tins. In a large glass, china or plastic bowl mix the two flours, salt, brown sugar and xanthan gum. Stir in the easy-blend yeast completely before making a well in the centre of the ingredients.

Gradually pour and mix in the water and 2 tbsp oil, carefully stirring in the dry ingredients from the edges of the flour well to form a smooth, well-blended, softish mixture. Unlike most of the breads in this book, the dough does not require any kneadings. Simply transfer the soft dough to the prepared tins, smooth the top and cover loosely with oiled clingfilm.

Leave to rise at a coolish room temperature, out of draughts, for about 2 hours until risen to the top of the tins.

Meanwhile, preheat the oven to 200°C (400°F/gas mark 6). Brush the tops of the loaves with the remaining oil and bake in the centre of the oven for about 40 minutes until risen, golden and crusty; the loaves should sound hollow when tapped underneath. Turn out onto a wire rack to cool.

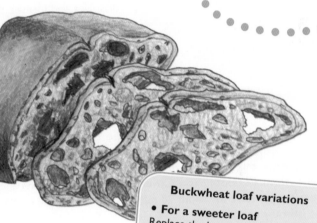

Buckwheat loaf variations

• For a sweeter loaf

Replace the brown rice flour with barley flour to give a sweeter loaf, or use gram flour for a more savoury flavour.

• Seedy top

Glaze the tops of the loaves with water before baking then scatter with lightly toasted sunflower, pumpkin or flax seeds and bake as above.

French baguettes

A unique style of bread with a crisp, golden crust and a deliciously airy and chewy crumb, traditionally, French baguettes are baked in specially shaped tins that give the rounded sides. Using baking trays will give you a flatter baked loaf.

Makes *two 350 g (12 oz) baguettes*

20 g (¾ oz) fresh yeast or
2½ tsp dried yeast

350 ml (12 fl oz) tepid water

500 g (1 lb 2 oz) white bread flour

1½ tsp salt

Fine cornmeal or extra flour to dust

Crumble the fresh yeast into a small glass bowl and add 200 ml (7 fl oz) of the tepid water. Using a wooden spoon, mix the yeast until it dissolves and forms a smooth paste. If using dried yeast, sprinkle yeast over the same amount of tepid water and proceed as for fresh yeast (also see page 46 in Techniques).

Mix the flour and salt in a large mixing bowl and make a well in the centre. Pour the yeasty liquid into the centre of the well, and using a wooden spoon, gently mix together with a little of the flour from the edges of the well to form a smooth paste. Cover with a clean tea towel and leave at room temperature for about 20 minutes until the paste forms a 'sponge' and is frothy and bubbling.

Gradually pour and mix in the remaining water, carefully stirring in the remaining dry ingredients from the edges of the flour well to form a softish, ball-like mixture in the middle. Turn the dough onto a lightly floured work surface and knead until smooth and elastic, about 10 minutes.

Put the dough in a lightly floured glass, china or plastic bowl big enough to allow the dough to double in size. Cover the bowl and leave to rise at a coolish room temperature out of draughts for 1½–2 hours until it has doubled in size.

Once it has risen satisfactorily, knock back and turn it out onto a lightly floured surface. Form the dough into a ball and let it rest for 5 minutes before you shape it.

Divide the dough into two equal pieces and form into long lengths of about 30 cm (12 in). Transfer to a large baking sheet lightly dusted with cornmeal or flour. Set aside for 5 minutes.

Using a sharp knife, slash the tops with diagonal slits about ½ cm (¼ in) deep, down the length of the dough, and brush the tops with cold water.

Place a large roasting tin of very hot water in the bottom of a cold oven and put the loaves on the middle shelf of the oven. Close the door and set the temperature to 200°C (400°F/gas mark 6). Bake the loaves for about 40 minutes until they are golden, crusty and sound hollow when tapped underneath. Transfer to a wire rack to cool. Best served warm.

French-style sourdough loaf

You need to make a starter for this recipe so plan ahead by several days; this the most traditional and natural way to leaven bread. You can use the basic starter recipe given on page 47.

Makes one 900 g (2 lb) ring-shaped loaf

400 g (14 oz) very strong white bread flour

100 g (3½ oz), plus 1 tbsp rye flour

1½ tsp salt

300 ml (10 fl oz) basic starter

175 ml (6 fl oz) tepid water

In a large glass, china or plastic bowl, mix the flours (reserving 1 tbsp rye flour) and salt. Make a well in the centre and add the starter (reserve and replenish the remaining starter as directed on page 47) and gently mix together using a wooden spoon with a little of the flour from the edges of the well to form a smooth paste.

Gradually pour and mix in the water, carefully stirring in the dry ingredients from the edges of the flour well to form a stiff, sticky ball-like mixture in the middle. Turn the dough onto a lightly floured work surface and knead until smooth and elastic, about 10 minutes.

Put the dough in a lightly floured glass, china or plastic bowl big enough to allow room for the dough to double in size. Cover the bowl and leave to rise at a coolish room temperature out of draughts for 1½–2 hours until doubled in size.

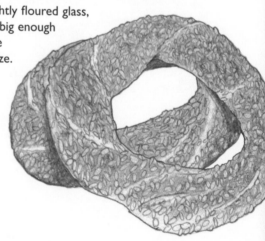

Once the dough has risen satisfactorily, knock back and turn it out onto a lightly floured surface. Form the dough into a ball and let it rest for about 5 minutes before you shape it.

To make a ring-shaped loaf, shape the dough into a round shape first as directed on page 54. Using the knuckles of your hand, push down firmly into the centre of the dough to make a hole.

Lightly push out the dough using stretched fingers to make a hole about 15 cm (6 in) in diameter. Transfer to a large lightly floured baking tray, cover loosely with oiled clingfilm and set aside to prove in a warm place until doubled in size.

Meanwhile, preheat the oven to 220°C (425°F/gas mark 7). Remove the cover, dust with reserved rye flour and bake in the centre of the oven for about 30 minutes until golden, risen and hollow-sounding when tapped underneath. Transfer the loaf to a wire rack to allow it to cool completely.

Sourdough variation

• Glaze the ring with water and liberally sprinkle the surface with sesame seeds before placing in the oven to bake (see left).

Ciabatta

As well as using a sourdough starter, you need to add a little yeast to the dough to make this popular aerated bread. The extra yeast quantity is very small, so is easier to use dried yeast.

Pour half the water into a small bowl and sprinkle over the dried yeast. Leave for about 5 minutes then stir to dissolve.

In a large glass, china or plastic bowl, mix the flour and salt. Make a well in the centre and add the yeasty liquid, the starter mixture (reserve and replenish the remaining starter as directed on page 47) and the olive oil. Gently mix together using a wooden spoon with a little of the flour from the edges of the well to form a smooth paste.

Makes two 350 g (12 oz) loaves

125 ml (4 fl oz) tepid water

½ tsp dried yeast

350 g (12 oz) white bread flour plus extra to dust

1½ tsp salt

300 ml (10 fl oz) basic starter (see page 47)

2 tbsp olive oil

Gradually pour and mix in the remaining water, carefully stirring in the dry ingredients from the edges of the flour well to form a sticky dough. This dough will be too soft to knead, so, without adding any flour, use your hand to twist, turn and stretch the dough the bowl, for about 5 minutes unt the mixture begins to pull away from the sides of the bowl. You may prefer to use a wooden spoon.

Cover the bowl with a clean tea towel or muslin (cheesecloth) and leave to rise at a coolish room temperature out of draughts for about 3 hours until three times the size. Do not push or mix the dough at all.

Dust two large baking trays generously with flour. Using a sharp knife, cut the dough in half. Flour your hands well and scoop out one half of the dough onto a baking tray. Shape the dough into an oblong about 25 cm (10 in) long, tucking the edges under, and neatening the sides with your fingers. Lightly dust the top with flour and leave uncovered to prove in a warm place for 20 minutes.

Repeat with the other half of the dough. Preheat the oven to 200°C (400°F/gas mark 6). Bake the loaves for about 30 minutes, swapping them round in the oven halfway through, until risen, golden and hollow sounding when tapped underneath. Transfer to a wire rack to cool.

German-style rye bread

Rye is an important cereal crop in Germany and there are many varieties of rye bread. I use a sourdough starter to make a dense, slightly sour-tasting loaf. Leave the caraway seeds out if preferred. This bread is a perfect partner for smoked salmon and other smoked fish and meats.

Makes one 23 cm (9 in) long loaf

350 g (12 oz) rye flour, plus extra for dusting

150 g (5½ oz) very strong bread flour

1½ tsp salt

2 tsp caraway seeds (optional)

300 ml (10 fl oz) sourdough starter (see page 47)

175 ml (6 fl oz) tepid water

In a large glass, china or plastic bowl, mix the flours, salt and seeds. Make a well in the centre and add the starter (reserve and replenish the remaining starter as directed on page 47) and gently mix together using a wooden spoon with a little of the flour to form a smooth paste.

Gradually pour and mix in the water, carefully stirring in the dry ingredients from the edges of the flour well to form a stiff, sticky ball-like mixture in the middle. Turn the dough onto a lightly floured work surface and knead until smooth and elastic, about 10 minutes.

Put the dough in a lightly floured glass, china or plastic bowl big enough to allow room for the dough to double in size. Cover the bowl and leave to rise at coolish room temperature or

of draughts for 1½–2 hours until doubled in size. As with all doughs using a sourdough starter, you may find that it takes longer than a couple of hours for the dough to actually double in size. Be patient; it will happen but starter-activated doughs don't rise quite so rapidly as those made with yeast.

Once the dough has risen satisfactorily, knock back and turn it out onto a lightly floured surface. Form the dough into a ball and let it rest for 5 minutes before you shape it into a 25 cm (10 in) long loaf as described on page 53. Carefully transfer to a large lightly floured baking tray, seam-side down, cover loosely with oiled clingfilm and set aside to prove in a warm place until doubled in size.

Meanwhile, preheat the oven to 200°C (400°F/gas mark 6). If you want, slash the loaf diagonally about 1 cm (½ in) deep down its length using a sharp knife. Or leave it as it is, dust lightly with rye flour and bake in the centre of the oven for about 45 minutes, until golden brown and hollow-sounding when tapped underneath. Transfer to a wire rack to cool.

Gluten-free sourdough

Follow the instructions for making a sourdough starter on page 47, but use ric
flour instead. The rest of the recipe uses a ready-blended gluten-free bread flo
which has xanthan gum added to it. You may like to experiment using your ow
favourite flours, adding xanthan gum as necessary.

Makes *two 600 g (1 lb 5 oz) loaves*

500 g (1 lb 2 oz) gluten-free bread flour

1 tsp salt

1 tbsp caster sugar

300 ml (10 fl oz) basic gluten-free sourdough starter (see page 47)

2 medium eggs, beaten

3 tbsp olive oil

275 ml (9½ fl oz) tepid water

Grease two 450 g (1 lb) loaf tins. In a large glass, china or plastic bowl, mix the gluten-free flour, salt and sugar and make a well in the centre. A the gluten-free starter that you've already made (you hav to think ahead with this recipe and any others that require a starter as a leavener), the eggs and 2 tbsp oil and gently mix together using a wooden spoon to form a smooth paste. Reserv and replenish the remaining starter as directed on page 47 an return to the refridgerator.

Gradually pour and mix in the water, carefully stirring in the dry ingredients from the edges of the flour well to form a sticky mixture. Unlike more conventional breadmaking, this recipe doesn't require any

kneading, so once the flour is well incorporated you can place it directly into the tins. Divide the dough equally and transfer to the prepared baking tins. Smooth the tops of the loaves, cover loosely with oiled clingfilm and leave to rise in a coolish room temperature out of draughts for about two hours until risen above the sides of the tin. Keep in mind that rising times may be slightly longer when using a sourdough starter rather than yeast.

Meanwhile, preheat the oven to 200°C (400°F/gas mark 6). Brush the tops of the loaves with the remaining oil and bake in the centre of the oven for about 40 minutes until risen, crusty and golden. The loaves will sound hollow when tapped underneath. Turn out onto a wire rack to cool.

Brioche à tête

A perfect brunch treat, this buttery enriched French loaf with its smaller crown topknot, is traditionally baked in a fluted tin. Brioche dough tends to be quite sticky, but avoid adding too much flour, otherwise you will affect the texture.

Crumble the fresh yeast into a small glass bowl and add the tepid water. Using a wooden spoon, mix the yeast until it dissolves and forms a smooth paste. If using dried yeast, sprinkle the dry yeast over the same amount of tepid water and proceed as for fresh yeast (also see page 47 in Techniques). I

Mix the flour, sugar and salt in a large mixing bowl and make a well in the centre.

Makes one 18 cm (7 in) diameter loaf

15 g (½ oz) fresh yeast or 2 tsp dried yeast
2 tbsp tepid water
250 g (9 oz) white bread flour
1 tbsp caster sugar
½ tsp salt
2 medium eggs, beaten
75 g (2½ oz) unsalted butter, very soft
1 egg yolk mixed with 1 tbsp water, to glaze

Pour the yeasty water in the centre of the flour well along with the beaten eggs and gently mix together using a wooden spoon, stirring in the dry ingredients from the edges of the flour well to form a soft, sticky ball-like mixture in the middle.

Turn the dough onto a lightly floured work surface and knead until smooth and elastic, about 10 minutes – it will become less sticky as you work the dough.

Grease a glass, china or plastic bowl with a small knob of the butter and put the dough in the bowl. The bowl needs to be big enough to allow the dough to double in size. Cover with a clean tea towel or muslin (cheesecloth) and leave to rise at a coolish room temperature out of draughts for about two hours until doubled in size.

Once the dough has risen satisfactorily, knock back and turn it out onto a lightly floured surface. Form the dough into a ball and let it rest for 5 minutes.

Flatten the dough slightly and then spread the top with 50 g (1¾ oz) of the remaining butter. Gradually work the butter into the dough by squeezing the dough with your hands. Knead for 3–4 minutes to make sure the butter is thoroughly blended throughout the dough, then form into a smooth round ball. Rest for 5 minutes.

Grease an 18 cm (7 in) diameter fluted brioche tin or a deep 16 cm (6 in) straight-sided round cake tin with the remaining butter. Cut off a quarter of the dough. Form the large piece into a ball as directed on page 54 and place it, seam-side down, in the prepared tin. Make an indentation on top in the centre using your finger. Brush the indent with a little of the egg yolk mixture.

Shape the small piece of dough into a round ball in the same way as above and place in the indent. Using a greased wooden spoon handle, push down straight through the centre of the top dough ball, pressing it onto the bottom piece to seal it securely in place. Cover loosely with oiled clingfilm and set the loaf aside to prove in a warm place for about 40 minutes until it has doubled in size.

Meanwhile, preheat the oven to 220°C (425°F/gas mark 7). Remove the covering and brush all over with beaten egg yolk. Bake in the centre of the oven for about 25 minutes until richly golden, well-risen and hollow-sounding when tapped underneath. Turn out onto a wire rack to cool. Brioche is best served warm.

Bagels

This famous Jewish bread roll is popular with everyone. Although best made and eaten as fresh as possible, they do freeze well – cool, wrap tightly and freeze for up to three months.

Makes *eight bagels*

15 g (½ oz) fresh yeast or 2 tsp dried yeast

275 ml (9½ fl oz) tepid water

550 g (1 lb 4 oz) white bread flour

2 tbsp caster sugar

2 tsp salt

2 tbsp vegetable oil

1 egg yolk mixed with 1 tbsp water, to glaze

2 tbsp poppy or sesame seeds (optional)

Crumble the fresh yeast into a small glass bowl and add 100 ml (3½ fl oz) of the tepid water. Using a wooden spoon mix the yeast until it dissolves and forms a smooth paste. If using dried yeast, sprinkle yeast over the same amount of tepid water and proceed as for fresh yeast (also see page 46 in Techniques).

Mix 500 g (1 lb 2 oz) flour, sugar and salt in a large mixing bowl and make a well in the centre. Pour the yeasty water into the centre of the well along with the oil and mix together using a wooden spoon with enough flour from the edges of the well to form a smooth paste.

Gradually pour and mix in the remaining water, carefully stirring in the dry ingredients from the edges of the flour well to form a firm, moist ball-like mixture in the middle of the bowl.

Generously flour the work surface with some of the remaining flour. Turn the dough onto it and knead until smooth and elastic, about 10 minutes, gradually adding all the remaining flour to make a very firm dough.

Put the dough in a lightly floured glass, china or plastic bowl big enough to allow room for the dough to double in size. Cover the bowl with a clean tea towel or muslin (cheesecloth) and leave to rise at a coolish room temperature out of draughts for about 1½ hours until doubled in size.

Once the dough has risen satisfactorily, knock back and turn it out onto a lightly floured surface. Form the dough into a ball and let it rest for about 5 minutes on the work surface.

Divide the dough into eight equal pieces and shape each into a smooth round. Lightly grease the end of a wooden spoon and press through the centre of each, wiggling the spoon around to stretch and enlarge the hole in the centre.

Carefully transfer to an oiled baking tray, spaced well apart, and cover with oiled clingfilm. Leave in a warm place to prove for about 20 minutes until just starting to rise – take care not to let the rings rise too much otherwise they will become misshapen. Open up the centre hole again if necessary using the wooden spoon handle.

Meanwhile, preheat the oven to 220°C (425°F/gas mark 7). Bring a large, deep-sided casserole or frying pan of water to the boil and reduce to a gentle simmer. Poach four bagels at a time for one minute on one side only. Remove with a slotted spoon and place on a large, lightly greased baking tray.

Brush the bagels all over with egg yolk glaze and sprinkle lightly with seeds if using. Bake in the centre of the oven for about 20 minutes, until richly golden. Transfer to a wire rack to cool. Best served warm, or split and lightly toasted, bagels are delicious with both savoury and sweet fillings.

Middle Eastern-style flat bread

Tastier than any pittas I've been able to buy, these much-loved flat breads are straightforward to make. They will keep quite well in a sealed plastic container for a few days – simply pop in the toaster for a few seconds to warm through before eating.

Makes *eight pittas*

15 g (½ oz) fresh yeast or 2 tsp dried yeast or 1¼ tsp easy-blend yeast

275 ml (9½ fl oz) tepid water

500 g (1 lb 2 oz) white bread flour

1 tsp salt

1 tsp caster sugar

4 tbsp olive oil

Crumble the fresh yeast into a small glass bowl and add 100 ml (3½ fl oz) of the tepid water. Usin a wooden spoon, mix the yeast until it dissolves and forms a smooth paste. If using dried yeast sprinkle yeast over the same amount of tepid water and proce as for fresh yeast (also see page in Techniques). If using easy-blend yeast, simply mix with your flour before adding any liquid.

Mix flour, salt and sugar in a large mixing bowl and make a well in the centre. Pour the yeasty water in the centre of the well along with 2 tbsp oil and gently mix together using a wooden spoon with a little of the flou from the edges of the flour well to form a smooth paste.

Gradually pour and mix in the remaining water, carefully stirring in the dry ingredients from the edges of the well to form a firmish, moist mixture in the middle. Turn the dough onto a lightly floured work surface and knead until smooth and elastic, about 10 minutes.

Put the dough in a lightly oiled glass, china or plastic bowl big enough to allow room for the dough to double in size. Cover the bowl with a clean tea towel or muslin (cheesecloth) and leave to rise at a coolish room temperature out of draughts for about 1½ hours, until doubled in size.

Once the dough has risen satisfactorily, knock back and turn it out onto a lightly floured surface. Form the dough into a ball and let it rest for 5 minutes.

Divide the dough into eight equal pieces and shape each piece into a smooth ball as described on page 54. Roll each piece into a thin oval shape about 20 cm (8 in) long. Transfer to lightly greased baking trays and cover with oiled clingfilm. Leave in a warm place to prove for about 20 minutes until just risen and slightly puffy.

Meanwhile, preheat the oven to 220°C (425°F/gas mark 7). Brush each bread generously with the remaining olive oil and bake for about 10 minutes until puffy and lightly golden. Best served warm.

Naan breads

Traditionally, these delicious flat breads are cooked in a tandoor oven to give them a quick blast of high heat and light charring. This recipe shows you how to get the same results using an ordinary oven and grill.

Crumble the fresh yeast into a small glass bowl and add 100 ml (3½ fl oz) of the tepid water. Using a wooden spoon, mix the yeast until it dissolves and forms a smooth paste. If using dried yeast, sprinkle yeast over the same amount of tepid water and proceed as for fresh yeast (also see page 46 in Techniques). If using easy-blend yeast, simply mix with your flour before adding any liquid.

Makes *four 25 cm (10 in) breads*

15 g (½ oz) fresh yeast or 2 tsp dried yeast or 1¼ tsp easy-blend yeast
150 ml (5 fl oz) tepid water
100 g (3½ oz) full-fat natural yoghurt
500 g (1 lb 2 oz) white bread flour
1½ tsp salt
1 tsp caster sugar
2 tsp black onion seeds, optional
75 g (2½ oz) ghee or butter, melted

Mix flour, salt, sugar and seeds in a large mixing bowl and make a well in the centre of the bowl. Pour the yeasty water in the centre of the well. Add the yoghurt and 4 tbsp melted ghee or butter. Gently mix together using a wooden spoon with a little of the flour from the well to form a smooth paste.

Gradually pour and mix in the remaining water, stirring in the dry ingredients from the edges of the well to form a firmish, moist mixture in the middle. Turn the dough onto a lightly floured work surface and knead until smooth and elastic, about 10 minutes.

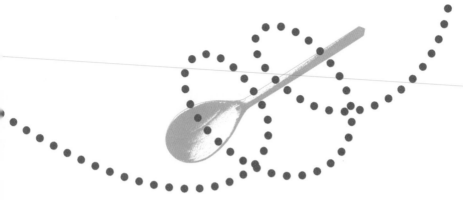

Put the dough in a lightly floured glass, china or plastic bowl big enough to allow room for the dough to double in size. Cover the bowl with a clean tea towel or muslin (cheesecloth) and leave to rise at a coolish room temperature out of draughts for about 1½ hours until doubled in size.

Once it has risen satisfactorily, knock back and turn it out onto a lightly floured surface. Form the dough into a ball and let it rest for 5 minutes on the work surface.

Preheat the oven to 240°C (475°F/gas mark 9). Divide the dough into four equal pieces and shape each piece into a smooth ball as described on page 54. Roll each piece into an oval shape about 25 cm (10 in) long.

Carefully lay two breads side by side on each baking tray and cook in the oven for 6 minutes until puffed up and browning round the edges.

Meanwhile, preheat the grill to its hottest setting. Carefully transfer the naan breads to the grill rack and continue to cook for about 30 seconds on each side until they brown and blister – make sure they aren't too close to the grill element or flames to avoid burning. Brush with the remaining melted ghee or butter and serve warm.

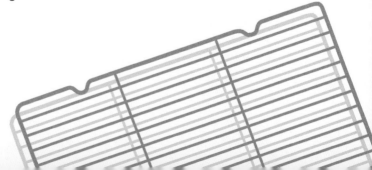

Panettone

This Italian Christmas bread is full of rich flavours, a sprinkling of fruit and peel with a half cake/half bread soft, airy texture. It is delicious both warm and cold, and is often presented tied up with a ribbon bow.

Makes one 20 cm (8 in) round loaf

25 g (1 oz) fresh yeast or 2¾ tsp dried yeast

200 ml (7 fl oz) tepid whole milk

400 g (14 oz) white bread flour

1 tsp salt

50 g (1¾ oz) caster sugar

115 g (4 oz) unsalted butter, softened

2 medium egg yolks

1 tsp vanilla extract

75 g (2½ oz) candied citrus peel, finely chopped

75 g (2½ oz) golden sultanas

Pinch of grated nutmeg

2 tsp icing sugar, to dust

Crumble the fresh yeast into a small glass bowl and add the tepid milk. Using a wooden spoon, mix the yeast until it dissolves and forms a smooth paste. using dried yeast, sprinkle yeast over the same amount of tepid milk and proceed as for fresh yeast (also see page 46 in Techniques).

Mix the flour, salt and sugar in a large mixing bowl and make a well in the centre. Pour the yeasty milk in the centre of the well, and gently mix together using a wooden spoon with a little of the flour to form a smooth paste. Cover with a clean tea towel and leave at room temperature for about 20 minutes until the paste forms a 'sponge' and is frothy and bubbling.

Mix in the flour from the sides of the sponge to form
a stiff dough. Turn the dough onto a lightly floured
work surface and knead until smooth and elastic,
about 10 minutes. Put the dough in a lightly oiled
glass, china or plastic bowl big enough to allow the
dough to double in size. Cover the bowl with a
clean tea towel or muslin (cheesecloth) and leave
to rise at a coolish room temperature out of
draughts for about 1½–2 hours until doubled in size.

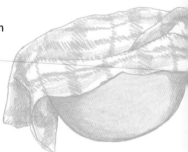

Once it has risen satisfactorily, knock back and turn it out onto a lightly
floured surface. Form the dough into a ball and let it rest for 5 minutes.

Grease and line a deep 20 cm (8 in) round cake tin. Lightly dust the work
surface with a little flour and flatten the dough out slightly. Spread the top
with butter. Put the egg yolks and vanilla in the middle and pile
the fruit and nutmeg on top. Fold the sides of
the dough over and carefully knead all the
ingredients together until well blended. The
mixture will be quite sticky until the
ingredients are well mixed.

Form into a ball as described on page 54,
and carefully lower into the tin, seam side down. Cover loosely with oiled
clingfilm and set aside to prove in a warm place for about an hour until
the middle of the dough is near the top of the tin.

Meanwhile, preheat the oven to 200°C (400°F/gas 6). Using a sharp knife,
cut a cross in the top of the dough about 1 cm (½ in) deep.

Bake in the centre of the oven for 10 minutes, then reduce the heat to
180°C (350°F/gas mark 4) and cook for a further 45 minutes until golden
and risen and a skewer inserted into the centre comes out clean. Turn out
onto a wire rack and leave to cool in the tin lining paper. Dust with icing
sugar and tie with ribbon to serve.

Doughnuts

Although widely available as a fast-food snack, the old-fashioned-style doughnut is still the best in my opinion. Crunchy sugar on the outside and fluffy dough on the inside, I add a pinch of spice to mine, but they are just as good left plain.

Makes *18 doughnuts*

25 g (1 oz) fresh yeast or
2¾ tsp dried yeast

175 ml (6 fl oz) tepid whole milk

500 g (1 lb 2 oz) white bread flour

1 tsp salt

50 g (1¾ oz) caster sugar, plus extra for dredging

½ tsp ground cardamom (optional)

50 g (1¾ oz) unsalted butter, melted

1 medium egg, beaten

Vegetable oil for deep frying

Crumble the fresh yeast into a small glass bowl and add half the milk. Using a wooden spoon, mix the yeast until it dissolves and forms a smooth paste. If using dried yeast, sprinkle yeast over the same amount of tepid milk and proceed as for fresh yeast (also see page 46 in Techniques).

Mix flour, salt, sugar and spice, if using, in a large mixing bowl and make a well in the centre of the flour. Pour the yeasty milk in the centre of the well. Add the butter and egg. Gently mix together using a wooden spoon with a little of the flour from the well to form a smooth paste.

Gradually pour and mix in the remaining milk, carefully stirring in the dry ingredients from the edges of the flour well to form a firmish, moist dough in the centre. Turn the dough onto a lightly floured work surface and knead until smooth and elastic, and the dough no longer sticks to the work surface, which should take about 10 minutes.

Put the dough in a lightly oiled glass, china or plastic bowl big enough to allow the dough to double in size. Cover the bowl with a clean tea towel or muslin (cheesecloth) and leave to rise at a coolish room temperature out of draughts for about 2 hours until doubled in size.

Once it has risen satisfactorily, knock back and turn it out onto a lightly floured surface. Form the dough into a ball and let it rest for 5 minutes.

Divide the dough into 18 pieces, and form each into a round as described on page 54. Flatten slightly, then arrange, well spaced out, on well-oiled baking trays. Cover with oiled clingfilm and set aside in a warm place to prove for 30–40 minutes until doubled in size.

Meanwhile, heat the oil for deep frying in a large saucepan to 180°C (350°F). Deep-fry four or five doughnuts in the hot oil for 5 minutes, turning them in the oil, until puffed up and richly golden brown. Drain well and then dredge in caster sugar while warm. Best eaten on the same day – delicious served warm.

Stollen

Another festive bread, this time from Germany. If you like marzipan, this is the recipe for you as there is a whole chunk of the stuff running down the centre of this fruited loaf. It keeps well – simply wrap and store for up to 5 days.

Makes one 23 cm (9 in) long bread

15 g (½ oz) fresh yeast or
2 tsp dried yeast

150 ml (5 fl oz) tepid whole milk

250 g (9 oz) white bread flour

1½ tsp ground mixed spice

½ tsp salt

25 g (1 oz) caster sugar

zest of 1 small unwaxed lemon

25 g (1 oz) unsalted butter

75 g (2½ oz) luxury dried fruit mix

150 g (5½ oz) marzipan

2 tsp icing sugar, to dust

Crumble the fresh yeast into a sma glass bowl and add the tepid milk. Using a wooden spoon, mix the yeast until it dissolves and forms smooth paste. If using dried yeas sprinkle yeast over the same amount of tepid milk and procee as for fresh yeast (also see page 46 in Techniques).

Put the flour, spice and salt in a bowl. Stir in the sugar and lemor zest and make a well in the cent of the flour. Pour the yeasty mill in the centre of the well and ad the melted butter. Gently mix together using a wooden spoo to make a softish dough. Turn onto a lightly floured surface and knead until smooth and elastic, for about 10 minutes.

Towards the end of the kneading time, flatten the dough slightly and pile the fruit on top, then fold over the dough and continue kneading until all the ingredients are well blended.

Put the dough in a lightly oiled glass, china or plastic bowl big enough to allow the dough to double in size. Cover the bowl with a clean tea towel or muslin (cheesecloth) and leave to rise at a coolish room temperature out of draughts for about 2 hours until slightly expanded – note this enriched dough will not rise quite as much as other mixtures.

Once it has risen satisfactorily, knock back and turn it out onto a lightly floured surface. Form the dough into a ball and let it rest for 5 minutes on the work surface. Roll the dough into an oval shape about 25 x 18 cm (10 x 7 in). Form the marzipan into a 23 cm (9 in) sausage shape and fit neatly down the length of the dough.

Carefully fold the dough over the marzipan and press the edges together all round to seal. Carefully transfer to a lightly greased baking tray. Cover loosely with oiled clingfilm and set aside in a warm place to prove for about 1 hour until slightly risen.

Meanwhile, preheat the oven to 200°C (400°F/gas mark 6). Bake in the centre of the oven for about 25 minutes until risen and golden brown. Transfer to a wire rack to cool. Dust with icing sugar before serving.

Walnut bread

Popular in the Mediterranean where this bread makes a good accompaniment to sharp-flavoured blue and goats' cheeses. I add a few raisins to the mixture leave them out if you prefer.

Makes one 900 g (2 lb) long loaf

15 g (½ oz) fresh yeast or
2 tsp dried yeast

300 ml (10 fl oz) tepid water

400 g (14 oz) very strong white bread flour

100 g (3½ oz) rye flour, plus extra to dust

1½ tsp salt

100 g (3½ oz) walnut pieces, roughly chopped

50 g (1¾ oz) raisins

Crumble the fresh yeast into a small glass bowl and add 100 ml (3½ fl oz) of the tepid water. Using a wooden spoon, mix the yeast until it dissolv and forms a smooth paste. If using dried yeast, sprinkle yeast over the same amount of tepid water and proceed as for fresh yeast (also see page 46 in Techniques).

Mix the flours and salt in a large mixing bowl and make a well in th centre of the flour. Pour the yeast liquid in the centre of the well, an gently mix together using a wood spoon with just a little of the flour to form a smooth paste. Cover with a clean tea towel and leave at room temperature for about 20 minutes until the paste forms a 'sponge' and is frothy and bubbling.

Gradually pour and mix in the remaining water, carefully stirring in the dry ingredients from the edges of the bowl to form a softish ball-like mixture in the middle. Turn onto a lightly floured surface and knead until smooth and elastic, about 10 minutes. Towards the end of the kneading time, flatten the

dough slightly and pile the walnuts and raisins on top, then fold over the dough and continue kneading until all of the ingredients are well blended.

Put the dough in a lightly oiled glass, china or plastic bowl big enough to allow the dough to double in size. Cover the bowl with a clean tea towel or muslin (cheesecloth) and leave to rise at a coolish room temperature out of draughts for about 1½–2 hours until doubled in size.

Once the dough has risen satisfactorily, knock back and turn it out onto a lightly floured surface. Form the dough into a ball and let it rest for about 5 minutes on the work surface.

Shape the dough into a 25 cm (10 in) long loaf as described on page 53. Transfer to a lightly floured baking tray, cover loosely with oiled clingfilm and set aside in a warm place to prove for about 40 minutes until about doubled in size.

Meanwhile, preheat the oven to 220°C (425°F/gas mark 7). Using a sharp knife, cut diagonal slashes about 1 cm (½ in) deep down the length of the loaf. Dust the top of the loaf with a little rye flour. Bake in the centre of the oven for about 30 minutes until risen, golden and hollow-sounding when tapped underneath. Transfer to a wire rack to cool.

Walnut bread variations

• Use chopped hazelnuts and dried prunes, or pecans, dried cherries and cranberries
• For a classic savoury bread, replace the dried fruit with roughly chopped pitted black olives

Pane al cioccolato

Italian chocolate bread is delicious cut into thin slices and spread with mascarpone or ricotta cheese. If you like nuts, replace the chocolate chips with chopped toasted hazelnuts, walnuts or almonds, or use dried fruit instead.

Makes *one 18 cm (7 in) round loaf*

15 g (½ oz) fresh yeast or 2 tsp dried yeast

275 ml (9¾ fl oz) tepid whole milk

425 g (15 oz) white bread flour

½ tsp salt

25 g (1 oz) cocoa powder

25 g (1 oz) dark brown sugar

25 g (1 oz) unsalted butter, melted

100 g (3½ oz) plain chocolate chips

1 egg white, beaten

1 tbsp caster sugar

Crumble the fresh yeast into a small glass bowl and add 100 ml (3½ fl oz) of the tepid milk. Using a wooden spoon, mix the yeast until it dissolves and forms a smooth paste. If using dried yeast, sprinkle yeast over the same amount of tepid milk and proceed as for fresh yeast (also see page 46 in Techniques).

Put the flour and salt in a bowl and sieve the cocoa on top. Stir in the brown sugar and make a well in the centre of the dry ingredients. Pour the yeasty milk into the centre of the well and add the melted butter. Gently mix together using a wooden spoon to form a smooth paste.

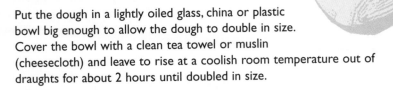

Gradually pour and mix in the remaining milk, stirring in the dry ingredients from the edge of the well to form a softish, ball-like mixture in the centre.

Turn onto a lightly floured surface and knead until smooth and elastic, about 10 minutes. Towards the end of the kneading time, flatten the dough slightly and pile the chocolate chips on top, then fold over the dough and continue kneading until all the ingredients are well blended.

Put the dough in a lightly oiled glass, china or plastic bowl big enough to allow the dough to double in size. Cover the bowl with a clean tea towel or muslin (cheesecloth) and leave to rise at a coolish room temperature out of draughts for about 2 hours until doubled in size.

Once it has risen satisfactorily, knock back and turn it out onto a lightly floured surface. Form the dough into a ball and let it rest for 5 minutes on the work surface.

Shape the dough into a round loaf as described on page 54. Transfer to a lightly greased baking tray, cover loosely with oiled clingfilm and set aside in a warm place to prove for about an hour until doubled in size.

Meanwhile, preheat the oven to 200°C (400°F/gas mark 6). Remove the cover and brush the loaf with egg white. Sprinkle with caster sugar and bake in the centre of the oven for about 30 minutes until well risen, crusted with sugar and hollow-sounding when tapped underneath. Transfer to a wire rack to cool. This loaf is delicious served either warm or cold.

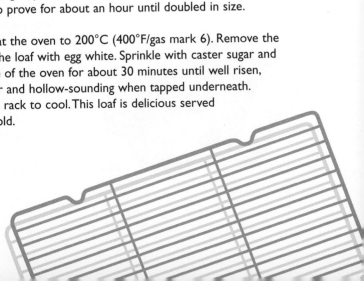

Potato bread

You can use all sorts of vegetables in your bread doughs. This basic reference recipe uses cold mashed potato and gives a moist, soft crumb to the finished loaf, but quite a number of root vegetables would be suitable alternatives. Try the suggestions listed at the end of the recipe.

Makes one 900 g (2 lb) tin loaf

15 g (½ oz) fresh yeast/2 tsp dried yeast

250 ml (9 fl oz) tepid water

350 g (12 oz) white bread flour

100 g (3½ oz) buckwheat flour

1½ tsp salt

2 tsp caster sugar

1½ tsp cumin seeds, crushed, plus extra for topping (optional)

100 g (3½ oz) smoothly mashed cold potato

2 tbsp olive oil

Crumble the fresh yeast into a small glass bowl and add 100 ml (3½ fl oz) of the tepid water. Using a wooden spoon, mix the yeast until it dissolves and forms a smooth paste. If you are using dried yeast, sprinkle the yeast over the same amount of tepid water and proceed as for fresh yeast (also see page 46 in Techniques).

Mix the flours, salt, sugar and cumin seeds, if using, in a large mixing bowl and make a well of dried ingredients in the centre. Pour the yeasty liquid into the centre of the well, and add the potato and 1 tbsp oil. Gently mix together using a wooden spoon with a little of the flour from the well to form a smooth paste.

Gradually pour and mix in the remaining water, carefully stirring in the dry ingredients from the edges of the well to form a soft ball-like mixture in the centre.

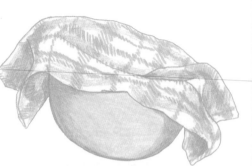

Turn onto a lightly floured surface and knead until smooth and elastic, about 10 minutes. This dough will be quite soft to work with due to the starchy potato; use extra flour sparingly and don't be tempted to added too much extra as it will give a dry texture to the finished loaf.

Put the dough in a lightly oiled glass, china or plastic bowl big enough to allow the dough to double in size. Cover the bowl with a clean tea towel or muslin (cheesecloth) and leave to rise at a coolish room temperature out of draughts for about 1½ hours until doubled in size.

Once it has risen satisfactorily, knock back and turn it out onto a lightly floured surface. It will still be quite soft. Form the dough into a ball and let it rest for 5 minutes on the work surface.

Shape the dough to fit the tin as described on page 54. Transfer to a lightly floured baking tin, cover loosely with oiled clingfilm and set aside to prove in a warm place for about 40 minutes until doubled in size.

Meanwhile, preheat the oven to 220°C (425°F/gas 7). Using a sharp knife, cut a slit in the top of the loaf about 1 cm (½ in) deep, brush with the remaining oil and sprinkle with seeds if using. Bake in the centre of the oven for about 30 minutes, until well-risen, golden brown and hollow-sounding when tapped underneath. Turn out onto a wire rack to cool.

Potato bread variations

- Replace the potato with smoothly mashed cooked beetroot and use caraway seeds to flavour
- Use smoothly mashed cooked parsnip or sweet potato with gram flour instead of buckwheat – add a pinch of dried chilli flakes for flavour
- For a carroty loaf, replace the water with carrot juice (leave out the sugar) and use 100 g (3½ oz) finely grated carrot instead of the mashed root vegetable – delicious made with all granary flour and a few ground coriander seeds for flavour.

Cheesy pesto swirl

A bread that's as good warm as it is cold so it is perfect for a special picnic sandwich. Delicious toasted too. The cornmeal gives it a firmer texture.

Crumble the fresh yeast into a small glass bowl and add 100 ml (3½ fl oz) of the tepid water. Using a wooden spoon, mix the yeast until it dissolves and forms a smooth paste. If using dried yeast, sprinkle yeast over the same amount of tepid water and proceed as for fresh yeast (also see page 46 in Techniques). If using easy-blend yeast, simply mix with your flour before adding any liquid.

Makes one 800 g (1 lb 12 oz) loaf

15 g (½ oz) fresh yeast or 2 tsp dried yeast or 1¼ tsp easy-blend yeast

275 ml (9½ fl oz) tepid water

350 g (12 oz) very strong white bread flour

100 g (3½ oz), plus 2 tsp fine cornmeal

1 tsp salt

75 g (2½ oz) finely grated fresh Parmesan cheese

2 tbsp red pesto

1 egg, beaten, to glaze

Mix the flour with the cornmeal and salt in a large mixing bowl. Stir in the cheese and make a well in the centre with the dry ingredients. Pour the yeasty liquid in the centre of the well and mix together using a wooden spoon with a little of the flour to form a smooth paste.

Gradually pour and mix in the remaining water, carefully stirring in the dry ingredients from the edges of the well to form a softish ball-like mixture in the centre. Turn onto a lightly floured surface and knead until smooth and elastic, for about 10 minutes.

Put the dough in a lightly floured glass, china or plastic bowl big enough to
allow the dough to double in size. Cover the bowl with a clean tea towel
or muslin (cheesecloth) and leave to rise at a coolish room temperature
out of draughts for about 1½–2 hours until doubled in size.

Once it has risen satisfactorily, knock back and turn it out onto a lightly
floured surface. Form the dough into a ball and let it rest for 5 minutes
on the work surface.

Grease and line a 900 g (2 lb) loaf tin. Press and roll the dough to make a
rectangular shape. Spread with pesto sauce right to the edge then roll up
like a Swiss roll.

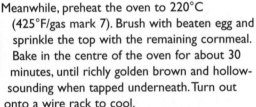

Carefully tuck the ends of the
dough underneath so that the
overall length fits neatly in the tin,
then transfer to the tin, seam-side
down. Cover loosely with oiled clingfilm
and set aside to prove in a warm place until
doubled in size.

Meanwhile, preheat the oven to 220°C
(425°F/gas mark 7). Brush with beaten egg and
sprinkle the top with the remaining cornmeal.
Bake in the centre of the oven for about 30
minutes, until richly golden brown and hollow-
sounding when tapped underneath. Turn out
onto a wire rack to cool.

Cheesy pesto variation

- Add 50 g (1¾ oz) finely chopped
cooked smoked bacon or the same
amount of drained tinned sweetcorn
kernels to the dough. For a smoky
flavour, add 1–2 tsp smoked paprika.

Soda bread

This spelt soda bread is one of my favourites. It's an easy recipe to adapt to make a wholewheat version, a classic white wheat flour loaf or add 75 g (2½ oz) chopped dried fruit for a sweeter loaf.

Makes one 750g (1lb 10oz) 20 cm (8 in) round loaf

450 g (1 lb) white spelt flour, plus extra for dusting

1 tsp salt

1 tsp bicarbonate of soda

1 tbsp caster sugar, optional

350 ml (12 fl oz) buttermilk

Preheat the oven to 220°C (425°F/gas mark 7). Lightly dust a large baking tray with flour.

Sieve the flour, salt and soda into a bowl and add any of the wheat husks that remain behind in the sieve. Stir in the sugar if using. Make a well in the centre. Pour most of the buttermilk in the centre of the well and gently mix together using your hands to make a softish mixture, adding more milk if necessary. Turn the mixture onto a lightly floured work surface and work it gently to tidy up the edges and neaten it.

Carefully transfer the mixture to the prepared baking sheet and press it down to make a round shape approximately 2.5 cm (1 in) thick. Using a sharp knife, cut a deep cross in the top, right to the edges. Bake in the centre of the oven for 15 minutes then reduce the heat to 200°C (400°F/gas mark 6) and continue to bake for a further 25 minutes until risen, golden and hollow-sounding when tapped underneath. Transfer to a wire rack to cool. Best eaten on day of baking.

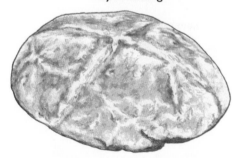

Soda bread tips

Buttermilk is available in low-fat and full-fat varieties, so choose whichever you prefer or make your own. Mix 3 tbsp fresh lemon juice into 650 ml (22 fl oz) full-fat milk. Leave at room temperature for 15 minutes, then cover and chill for up to 2 days. Stir before using.

merican-style cornbread

Perfect for mopping up soups, chillis and stews, this non-yeasted bread can be made up in no time and is absolutely delicious.

Makes *one 20 cm (8 in) square loaf*

150 g (5½ oz) plain flour

150 g (5½ oz) fine cornmeal

1 tsp bicarbonate of soda

1 tsp baking powder

1 tbsp caster sugar

2 medium eggs, beaten

25 g (1 oz) unsalted butter, melted

300 ml (10 fl oz) buttermilk

Preheat the oven to 200°C (400°F/gas mark 6). Grease a deep 20 cm (8 in) square tin. Sieve the flour, cornmeal, bicarbonate of soda, baking powder and sugar into a bowl and make a well in the centre. Add the eggs and melted butter and mix together using a wooden spoon.

Gradually mix in the buttermilk to make a smooth, thick batter. Transfer to the prepared tin and bake in the centre of the oven for about 25 minutes until golden and risen, and a skewer inserted into the centre comes out clean. Turn onto a wire rack to cool. Best served warm, cut into 12 squares.

Cornbread variation

• For an enhanced corn flavour, stir 115 g (4 oz) cooked sweetcorn kernels into the batter before baking.

Useful addresses

GENERAL (UK)

Flour Advisory Bureau (FAB)
21 Arlington Street
London SW1 1RN
Tel: +44 (0) 2074932521
www.fabflour.co.uk

The place to go for all things 'bread'. FAB has been providing information on all matters relating to flour and bread in the UK to the public, media, schools, health professionals and trade since the 1950s.

MILLERS AND FLOUR PRODUCERS (UK)

Bacheldre Mill
Churchstoke, Montgomery
Powys, Wales SY15 6TE
Tel: +44 (0)1588 620489
Fax: +44 (0)1588 620105
www.bacheldremill.co.uk

A traditional Welsh mill built on the site of an ancient watermill. Bacheldre Mill produces a wide range of organic bread and stonegrain flours as well as some specialities such as malted, spelt, rye and smoked; they also stock organic dried yeast and baking powder. Their flours are available mail order and via an online shop.

Doves Farm Foods Ltd
Salisbury Road
Hungerford, Berkshire
RG17 0RF
Tel: +44 (0)1488 684880
Fax: +44 (0)1488 685235
www.dovesfarm.co.uk

Specialists in organic and gluten-free flours and baking products such as buckwheat, spelt, gram, rye and rice flour as well as dried yeast, easy-blend dried yeast, xanthan gum and bicarbonate of soda. Products widely distributed throughout the UK as well as available mail order and via Doves Farm's online shop.

Shipton Mill Ltd
Long Newnton, Tetbury
Gloucestershire, GL8 8RP,
Tel: 01666 505050
Email: enquiries@shipton-mill.com
www.shipton-mill.com

Cotswolds mill providing quality bread and cake flour. Range includes wholewheat and white bread flours as well as rye, spelt, buckwheat and a speciality range. Products available mail order and via Shipton Mill's online shop.

Clarks (Wantage) Ltd
Wessex Mill, Mill Street
Wantage OX12 9AB,
Tel: +44 (0) 1235 768991
Fax: +44 (0) 1235 768993
www.wessexmill.co.uk

Wessex mill is a small mill, roller milling wheat since th early twentieth century. Products include wholewhe and white bread flours, gra rye, spelt and gluten-free flours. Products available m order and via Wessex Mill's online shop.

W & H Marriage & Sons L
Chelmer Mills, New Street
Chelmsford, Essex CM1 1P
Tel: + 44 (0) 1245 354455
Fax: + 44 (0) 1245 261492
www.marriagesmillers.co.uk

Large-scale millers of bread flours, based in Essex, and established in 1824. As well standard white and brown bread flours, Marriages also produces stoneground and organic flours. Their quality flours are widely distributed throughout the UK.

Carr's Flour Mills Ltd
Old Croft, Stanwix
Carlisle CA3 9BA
Tel: +44 (0)1228 554600
Fax: +44 (0)1228 554602
www.carrs-flourmills.co.uk

Large-scale millers with
factories in Essex, Scotland
and Cumbria. Carr's produce
a wide range of bread flours
including a malted range. Their
quality flours are widely
distributed throughout the
UK.

**ONLINE FRESH YEAST
SUPPLIERS (UK)**

www.nifeislife.com
An Italian online deli based in
north London sells fresh
yeast in 25 g cubes mail order

www.scandikitchen.co.uk
A Scandinavian online food
and general supplier based in
central London sells 50 g
packets fresh yeast mail order

www.thebertinetkitchen.com
'hirondelle' 500 g packets
fresh yeast (see more details
under bakeware)

**BAKEWARE AND
SPECIALIST EQUIPMENT
AND TINS (UK)**

Armorica
19 Rams Walk, Petersfield
Hants, GU32 3JA
Tel: +44 (0) 8456 017 262
Email:enquiries@armorica.co.
uk
www.armorica.co.uk

Cookshop based in
Petersfield, Hampshire with
online and mail order service.
French bread tins and other
bakeware.

The Bertinet Kitchen
12 St Andrew's Terrace
Bath BA1 2QR
Tel: +44 (0) 1225 445531
Email:
info@thebertinetkitchen.com
www.thebertinetkitchen.com

Bath based cookery school
with online bread baker's
cook shop. Online and mail
order specialist equipment as
well as fresh yeast.

de Cuisine
Spion House, Rushall Lane
Lytchett Matravers, Poole
Dorset BH16 6AJ
Tel: +44 (0) 1202 621472
Email via online web query
system
www.decuisine.co.uk –

Dorset based mail order and
online cook shop selling a
wide range of tins, bakeware
and specialist equipment such
as panettone tins.

Lakeland
Alexandra Buildings,
Windermere, Cumbria
LA23 2BQ
Tel: +44 (0) 15394 88100
Fax: +44 (0) 15394 88300
www.lakeland.co.uk

Online, mail order and retail
kitchenware and household
items. Wide selection of
bakeware and tins.

Legend Cookshops
27 High Street
Hythe, Kent
CT21 5AD
Tel: +44 (0) 1303 266300
Email:
sales@legendcookshop.co.uk
www.legendcookshop.co.uk

Online, mail order and retail
kitchen shop based in Kent.
Wide selection of tins and
bakeware as well as brioche
and French bread tins.

INTERNATIONAL INGREDIENT AND EQUIPMENT CONTACTS

www.williams-sonoma.com
Online and over 250 stores all over US and Canada with facilities to ship to over 75 countries. Speciality retailer in gourmet cookware and homeware, including French bread pans and other baking pans and trays.

www.pleasanthillgrain.com
Nebraska-based online suppliers of quality baking ingredients and bakeware including yeast and French bread pans.

www.amazon.com
Search engine facility offering wide selection of equipment available online from various suppliers.

INTERNATIONAL MILLING AND FLOUR INFORMATION SOURCES

Canadian National Millers Association
Suite 200
265 Carling Avenue
Ottawa, Canada
KIS 2EI
www.canadianmillers.ca

North American Millers Association
600 Maryland Avenue, SW,
Suite 825 West
Washington, DC 20024
www.namamillers.org

San Francisco Baking Institute
480 Grandview Drive
South San Francisco, CA 94080
www.sfbi.com

Wheat Food Council
51 D Red Fox Lane
Ridgway, CO 81432
www.wheatfoods.org

Association Nationale de Meunerie Française
66, rue La Boétie
F - 75008 Paris (France)
www.meuneriefrancaise.co

Italmopa
Associazione Industriali
Mugnai d'Italia
00198 Roma - Via Lovanio,
(Italy)
www.italmopa.com

Index